TIM STAFFORD

SURPRISED BY JESUS

His Agenda for Changing Everything
in A.D. 30 and Today

IVP Books

An imprint of InterVarsity Press
Downers Grove, Illinois

InterVarsity Press
P.O. Box 1400, Downers Grove, IL 60515-1426
World Wide Web: www.ivpress.com
E-mail: mail@ivpress.com

InterVarsity Press® is the book-publishing division of InterVarsity Christian Fellowship/USA®, a student movement active on campus at hundreds of universities, colleges and schools of nursing in the United States of America, and a member movement of the International Fellowship of Evangelical Students. For information about local and regional activities, write Public Relations Dept., InterVarsity Christian Fellowship/USA, 6400 Schroeder Rd., P.O. Box 7895, Madison, WI 53707-7895, or visit the IVCF website at <www.intervarsity.org>.

All Scripture quotations, unless otherwise indicated, are taken from the Holy Bible, New International Version®. NIV®. Copyright ©1973, 1978, 1984 by International Bible Society. Used by permission of Zondervan Publishing House. All rights reserved.

Design: Cindy Kiple
Images: Alinari/Art Resource, NY

ISBN-10: 0-8308-3340-4
ISBN-13: 978-0-8308-3340-5

Printed in the United States of America ∞

Library of Congress Cataloging-in-Publication Data

Stafford, Tim, 1950-
  Surprised by Jesus: his agenda for changing everything in A.D. *30*
  and today / Tim Stafford.
     p. cm.
  Includes bibliographical references and index.
  ISBN-13: 978-0-8308-3340-5 (cloth: alk. paper)
  ISBN-10: 0-8308-3340-4 (cloth: alk. paper)
  1. Jesus Christ—Person and offices. I. Title
  BT203.S72 2006
  232—dc22

                                                                  2006004132

P	18	17	16	15	14	13	12	11	10	9	8	7	6	5	4	3	2	1
Y	21	20	19	18	17	16	15	14	13	12	11	10	09	08	07	06			

To
Chase

CONTENTS

THE DECEPTIVELY
FAMILIAR JESUS

AS A BOY I LEARNED TO FISH IN A see-through river. Trout were so visible in the transparent water of the Big Sur that I could watch them approach, mouth and spit out my bait. I could lay down my line just in front of them, seeing them startle when the splash came too close. The sight of their gray shadows wavering across a forest pool made my boy heart pound. Each morning of vacation I woke with one objective: to find the fish and to catch them.

Even in such clear water, trout can easily fool the eye. The water is transparent, but it moves and bends light. A ripple, a rock, a well-placed stick can deceive. In water the fish do not look like the rounded, bright-colored images you find pictured in a guidebook. They are slim, elusive ghosts. A fisherman needs a practiced eye to read the water and see the fish.

For me, seeing Jesus in the Gospels is a little like that. The prose is clear water. Matthew, Mark, Luke and John concentrate on facts, telling who, what, when, where and how. Nevertheless, Jesus remains hard to grasp. I read the Gospels for a long time and never felt that I knew him in the way I felt I knew Martin Luther King Jr. or C. S. Lewis after I read their biographies and letters.

Everybody knows what it's like to look at some long-familiar object and see it as though for the first time. Perhaps it's a picture that hung in your living room since you were a child. Perhaps it's the house across the street, so familiar you have never really noticed it. Jesus is like that: deceptively familiar. People think they know all about him, so they never really look at him. When they finally do, they are surprised at what they find. Jesus may seem to be a stranger, even though they have grown up in his company.

"Deceptively familiar." We know absolutely nothing about Jesus' true appearance, yet oddly, his "portrait" can be put on a ten-second television spot and achieve one hundred percent name recognition. Jesus with the long hair, the flowing robe and the kind face can be portrayed by a hundred different artists and yet remain instantly recognizable.

Along with this visible portrait go personality attributes that "everybody knows." Jesus, everybody knows, was the kindest man who ever lived. Love spilled from him like the glow of a lamp. Children flocked to him; followers could get lost in the deep pools of compassion they met in his eyes. He was gentle and quiet. He felt others' pain deeply.

We know this Jesus so well that the question, "What would Jesus do?" seems to make perfect sense. (I can't always predict what my best friend will do, but I imagine that I know Jesus' behavior better than that.)

We feel we know Jesus because he's part of the landscape of our culture. Some of what we know, however, is based more on sentiment than on gospel truth.

When I first began to read the Gospels for myself, I didn't find this predictable, well-known Jesus. In the Gospels he says and does puzzling things—like shriveling a fig tree and telling followers to keep his miracles a secret. He's hard on people, excoriating the Pharisees and even calling one of his disciples "Satan." He makes extreme demands—like urging his followers to be as perfect as the Father in heaven—and exerts very little effort to explain himself. Jesus follows an agenda that his own followers, let alone the crowds, do not "get." Luke comments, "The disciples did not understand any of this. Its meaning was hidden from them, and they did not know what he was talking about" (Luke 18:34). Jesus in the Bible is much more difficult to make out than the universal Jesus whose kindness everybody knows.

Yet surely we are meant to understand the Jesus of the Bible. Surely that's why the early Christians carefully recorded the details of his life: so we could know him and follow him—indeed, so we could worship him.

Jesus Without His Context

Many Christians, if you asked them to tell you what they know about Jesus, would give a short summary that comes mainly from Paul's letters. It goes like this: Jesus is God, and he came to earth as a baby. He lived a sinless life and gave himself to die on the cross for our sins. Then he rose again and now lives in heaven.

Notice that in this telling, we don't need to know much about Jesus' life as the Gospels describe it. We know the beginning and the ending, but not much in between. Jesus did not sin, we know, but what he did do we can hardly explain. We say nothing about his teaching and healing and calling disciples. He could have been crucified anywhere and anytime—in Havana, Los Angeles or Beijing—and his atonement for sin would be the same.

Paul knew much more about Jesus than this brief summary suggests, and I believe he expected his readers to know more as well.
However, this was almost the only Jesus I knew as a young believer—
a Jesus without a context. In the background behind Jesus I could see
flat-roofed houses and Roman soldiers, but these were just stage
scenery. Jesus' life in the first century among an oppressed people under a Roman governor was irrelevant to his ministry, as far as I knew.

In church I learned that Jesus came "in the fullness of time" because the Roman Empire built good roads and spread the Greek language. Apparently the Roman Empire mattered because of its information infrastructure. (Never explained was why Jesus didn't come
later, after the invention of television.) Jesus' message addressed
nothing specific to the society he lived in, and certainly nothing to
the venomous power clash between Israel and Rome. He was a religious figure, and everybody knows that religion shouldn't meddle
with politics. Jesus spoke of eternal truths: heaven and peace with
God and love for your neighbor. Apparently he could have done the
same at any time, in any place.

Let me give a parallel example. Suppose I tried writing about the
wisdom of Abraham Lincoln without noting that he was president
during the Civil War. Can we admire the man without all that military history? I could compose quite a helpful book about Lincoln's
wit and wisdom without mentioning the war. I could show Lincoln
as philosophical, stirring, full of clever sayings—a kind of cracker-
barrel philosopher.

Yet I would give a very superficial portrayal of Lincoln unless I
showed how his wisdom led America through its most awful, bloody
crisis. To understand Lincoln as a wise man, and to grasp the depth
of his words, I must follow him through Bull Run, Shiloh, Gettysburg
and Appomattox. I must understand that the survival of "govern-

ment of the people, by the people, for the people" was at stake. I must grasp Lincoln's strategy for saving America.

It's the same with Jesus. If we settle for a superficial understanding of who he was and what he intended, we end up preaching a superficial gospel. The "everybody knows" version of Jesus too easily carries an individualistic, consumer-oriented appeal. In the extreme, we preach a gospel that is all about me—my personal growth, my spiritual experiences with Jesus as my friend. This makes worship superficial, for we miss the grandeur of Jesus' character and ministry.

Jesus would never have recognized faith lived apart from history and place and neighbors—and neither will we, if we are grounded in his life.

JESUS THE JEW

For almost forty years I have studied the Gospels. I have read and reread them trying to learn to see Jesus. Many writers, pastors and fellow believers—more than I could name—have aided me. In recent years I have been especially challenged and helped by the scholarly work known as the Third Quest, and particularly by the writings of N. T. Wright. Those familiar with Wright's work will see how frequently I have drawn on his scholarship.

Nothing I have learned makes me doubt the faith I gained as a child. However, I have found a great deepening in my understanding of Jesus. I feel as though I had been studying a picture in a book, and now the figure has begun to take on three dimensions and move as a living, breathing creature.

In particular, Wright has helped me understand Jesus as a first-century Jew. Of course, I always knew Jesus was Jewish, but the significance of that fact was vague to me. I suppose I inferred a meaning similar to Jewishness in twentieth-century America. I thought Jesus must have had dark eyes and hair and strong family ties. He ate kosher food and worshiped in a synagogue. None of these qualities seemed very important. Perhaps they added some color to Jesus' character, but they didn't clarify much about what he was doing. He could just as well have been Chinese or African or Anglo or Anything.

I did not understand that Jesus was a Jew in a sense that has largely vanished from the world today. Like many Jews of the first century, Jesus saw reality through the lens of the Hebrew Bible. Jesus believed the Scriptures, not only in the reverential way that religious believers typically "believe" in sacred texts, but in the sense that he thought they were true, true as the morning news, true as gravity. Those Scriptures explained what God had been doing since creation, and what he intended to do. The Hebrew Bible told Jews an astonishing story: any hope for the world would flow through them. They were God's chosen people, his instrument of redemption for all of creation. The whole world mattered to God, but the Jews mattered the most because he would use them to save the rest.

Jesus worked from the conviction that Israel had been called to restore the whole world. He also worked from the conviction that Israel could restore the world only as Israel was herself restored. Jesus came to Israel at a time when the nation was militarily occupied and culturally under siege. Within a generation, conquering armies would sweep it off the map. Sacrificial worship would come to an end as the temple—God's throne on earth—was destroyed. How could Israel save the world if temple and kingdom disappeared? Jesus came to this impending crisis—the hope of the world in the clutches of sin, the hope of the world on the edge of destruction. You cannot understand the eternal significance of what Jesus did unless you first understand the emergency he addressed among his own people in that time and place.

As any Bible reader knows, the Gospels claim that Jesus' life fulfilled many Old Testament prophecies. I used to understand those fulfillments as miraculous proofs to be checked off. Scripture predicted that the Messiah would be born in Bethlehem. Check! Scripture said that he would be born of a virgin. Check! Scripture predicted that the Savior of the world would ride into Jerusalem on a donkey. Check! This is like doing a crossword puzzle and seeing the answers fall neatly into place. It is scarily wonderful how the prophetic predictions came true. Somebody planned this!

But gradually I came to understand prophecies at a deeper level. The Old Testament texts are not checklists. They tell a story in which the entire cosmos is being reclaimed by God through one tiny nation's redemption. Jesus believed this incredible story. Jesus intended to bring the long story of Israel to a new era of fulfillment. That is how he fulfilled prophecies: he filled them full. The prophets glimpsed from afar the bright lights at the end of the story. Jesus began to switch on those lights.

As I have begun to understand Jesus in his first-century Jewish context, I have found his life imbued with depth and astonishing majesty. Everything I knew before seems to have gained new dimension and color and texture. I see a great, profound leader.

And as a result of seeing Jesus more clearly, I see my life—and human life—as deeper and grander. I see myself not as an isolated individual, a religious consumer who gets pleasurable spiritual experiences through Jesus. Rather I see myself bound into his family, joining in his astonishing flesh-and-blood mission to redeem the cosmos. I am part of a four-thousand-year-old movement that has outlasted empires and will, in the end, assume the administration of everything.

How I see Jesus is not a small thing, not a matter of my "spirituality."

Rather it is a matter of life—my own life and all life on the planet. To
see Jesus clearly and fully is ultimately to see everything. It is the
transforming core of vision. "In your light we see light" (Psalm 36:9).

                        *   *   *

Enough grand generalities. To see Jesus clearly we must study
what he said and did. The rest of this book will do just that. We will
follow Jesus through his ministry on earth: his baptism, his temptations, his preaching, his healings and works of power, his warnings,
his calling and sending of disciples, his praying, his death and resurrection. We will consider his time and place in history. We will locate
him in the historic community of Judaism.

We will also ask how each aspect of his ministry should affect our
lives today. Jesus very deliberately set out to start a movement. We are
part of that movement if we belong to him. We walk "in his steps," as
1 Peter 2:21 tells us. We will try to understand how Jesus' life guides
our lives in the movement he began. We will see the path he traveled
and then ask: how do we follow in his steps?

2

WHY REPENTANCE?
FOR WHAT SINS?

WHEN WE BEGIN TO LOOK FOR JESUS in the Gospels, our view gets blocked immediately. John the Baptist stands in the way. All four Gospels begin the story of Jesus' ministry with this eccentric figure, Jesus' cousin, who made a dramatic splash in Israel just before Jesus went to work.

In my Bible reading, I never really understood John, and I certainly didn't see why the Gospels began Jesus' ministry by telling about John. I also couldn't see why he provoked such a remarkable national response, with crowds of people hurrying out of town to find him in the wilderness. In the Gospels he comes across as a fire-breather. Why would crowds be attracted to that?

Most importantly, I had no idea why Jesus came to John for the "baptism of repentance for the forgiveness of sins" (Luke 3:3). Why would Jesus do that if he was sinless? Why repentance? For what sins?

Apparently the early Christians who wrote the Gospels saw John as extraordinarily important. In order to "get" Jesus, they thought we needed to "get" John. I could wish to skip over this beginning, seeking easier material. I have come to believe, though, that understanding Jesus' baptism by John is crucial for understanding the rest of Jesus' life. Through understanding John we can grasp Jesus' times and the context in which he worked.

You may find it tedious to discuss at length the meaning of John's baptism, since it does not seem to connect immediately to our lives. In fact, it may seem like ancient and dusty history, quite irrelevant. But bear with me. I think you will find John's baptism to be a key to everything that follows in Jesus' life. It opens many doors. And remember—if you grow impatient—that it was not my choice to begin here. It was Jesus' choice. It was the Gospel writers' choice. They all began with John and his baptism. If you don't understand why, what will you miss?

A STRANGE MAN

Who and what is John the Baptist? Holding no job and having no official position, John dressed in caveman clothing and lived off the land. He chose to preach not in the cities, where he could have found a ready audience, but in the wilderness. Such a person preaching along a rural highway today would cause people to speed up and lock the car doors, not rush out to hear him. We design homeless shelters for people like John.

In Jesus' day, however, John fit a more honorable profile. He was a "prophet"—a category well known then but almost forgotten today. Israel had an ancient traditional belief that God spoke to his people through prophets. Throughout Israel's history, prophets appeared before kings and people with a message from God. In Israel, people listened to prophets more or less in the way people today listen to stock market analysts.

Prophets made predictions, but more often they hammered on contemporary events. God's eternal law, the Torah, was precious to Israel, but it did not always tell them how to understand the challenges of the day. New enemies arose. Leaders good and bad came to power. Droughts, plagues and wars afflicted Israel. Choices had to be made—moral choices, economic choices, political choices. Prophets gave God's view. They often focused on sins that needed correction.

Since prophets spoke bluntly about current events, they frequently provoked controversy and persecution. Jeremiah, for example, told Israelites that it was futile to resist the Babylonian invaders. For his pains, he was called a traitor and thrown in prison, where he nearly died. John's life would follow a similar trajectory. For criticizing the government, he would be arrested, imprisoned and executed.

People in John's day desperately wanted to learn what God thought of their times. It had been generations since a bona fide prophet had been seen in Israel, but the prophets' voices inhabited Israelites' imaginations like ghosts. They believed in prophets even though they had never seen one. When John came claiming to speak for God, the masses hurried out to hear him in unprecedented eagerness. They would listen to Jesus for exactly the same reason. They had wrapped their national identity around God, their nation was in trouble, and they needed to know what God said. As a Scripture-saturated people they remembered that prophets had come from God in times of crisis. They believed—they hoped—they prayed—that prophets would come again.

GREAT GOOD NEWS

John provoked a seismic reaction with a simple announcement: "Repent, for the kingdom of heaven is near" (Matthew 3:2). Jesus would shortly begin to preach an identical message. Unfortunately, it is cryptic to us. What on earth did John mean, "The kingdom of heaven [or the kingdom of God] is near," and why did it provoke a mass reaction? Why would Jesus take up the same message?

The message is cryptic because it assumes that its hearers have been eagerly following a story. As N. T. Wright points out,

> These statements . . . are like saying, "Frodo and Sam have reached Mount Doom," or "They're coming into the home straight," or "Jayne has had her baby"; the hearer is assumed to know the context, the previous acts in the drama. To say "the kingdom of god is at hand" makes sense only when the hearers know "the story so far" and are waiting for it to be completed.

We run into such communication breakdowns all the time. Perhaps I'm lounging on the sofa listening to a baseball game when my wife says huffily to me, "They'll be arriving any minute." Her tone is urgent, but she doesn't realize that I wasn't listening when she told me our out-of-town guests were on their way. Without such background information my wife's message—and her emotions—completely mystify me.

Similarly, saying that the kingdom of God is near won't communicate to an audience that has no idea what the kingdom of God is and why we're waiting for it. Anywhere but in Israel, the phrase would be mystifying. No ordinary Gentile would have understood. "The kingdom of God" was neither a Greek nor a Roman concept. Homer, Plato and Aristotle spoke not a word about it. Only practicing Jews had the background to understand John's message. For them, the news was electric. They had been waiting for just such news all their lives.

THE STORY OF THE KINGDOM

"The story so far" was told in the Hebrew Scriptures: how God used

Abraham, Moses and David to create the kingdom of Israel and its remarkable hopes for life under God's care. Jews were raised to imagine
Abraham gazing at the night sky from beside his tent, hearing God
promise to make his family as numerous as the stars that spangled the
heavens. Jewish children surely felt their hearts pound as they listened to the story of Israelite slaves running from Pharaoh's army into
the desert. The story of the kingdom placed them waiting at the foot
of smoky Mount Sinai to see Moses descend carrying tablets of stone
with God's perfect law. They imagined fighting alongside David, the
youthful future king, as he battled giant Goliath to save the young
kingdom from foreign extermination.

The kingdom of God was a story, not a set of theological propositions. It had a tragic side: many prophets warning Israel that they
would forfeit God's blessing if they didn't stop abusing his love. The
terrible tale of Jerusalem's destruction, the burning of the temple, the
exile in Babylon and the torture and death of Israel's kings became
part of the story. The disgrace continued right up into Jesus' time, for
although Israel had come back from Babylonian captivity, they never
regained their political independence—that is, never again became a
kingdom.

By John's and Jesus' lifetimes, the story was poised on a painful dilemma. God's chosen people were still oppressed, still in the condition
of exile, still alienated from God by their sins. Yet God had promised
always to remain their God, their loving protector. He promised to
bring them back from exile, heal their wounds and restore their relationship to him. The prophets pointed toward a final resolution when
God would punish Israel's enemies. Israel's king would sit on the
throne again, raising the nation's peace and prosperity to such a level
that the whole world would submit to Jerusalem and worship Israel's
God. A reign of peace would come, with little Israel leading the entire

world. Lambs and lions would lie down lovingly together. Swords would be hammered into plows. The whole world would celebrate God's reign, with trees clapping their hands and the sea singing. In this new era—God's kingdom—God would judge dark and rebellious powers, exterminating disease and death. According to many Jews, the dead would come back to life, and the whole family of Israel, from Abraham on, would be united in the flesh for a great celebration.

God did not intend his people to remain a poor, oppressed nation under the domination of a foreign empire. He meant them to be the center of the universe, with himself as their center. Yet obviously God had not accomplished this yet. That was the story so far.

At this point in the story John appeared, saying, "Repent, for the kingdom of God is at hand."

John did not preach a sermon, as we usually think of sermons. He did not give a general perspective on the eternal ways of God. He brought news: the long-awaited day had come. Such an announcement would make any Jew with a shred of faith sit up and listen.

For a modern parallel, think about the fall of the Berlin Wall. At 6:53 p.m. on November 9, 1989, a member of the East German government was asked when a new open-border policy would begin. He answered: "Well, as far as I can see . . . straightaway, immediately." For twenty-eight years people had anticipated the day the wall would come down. Nevertheless, the announcement came as a shock. Suddenly, hope leaped to life in a million hearts.

Throughout Europe, people jumped into cars and trains to go see for themselves. Berliners jammed the subways and streets, racing to reach the wall. Soon the area was jammed with jubilant crowds singing, dancing and jabbering at each other in any language they shared. They found the wall undefended: no guards, no dogs, no guns. People boosted themselves up onto the top, which became too crowded for movement. Wine and beer passed from hand to hand among strangers. Perhaps five million people gathered and celebrated all night.

It was something like that for John the Baptist. In the fullness of time he made an announcement that set off a chain reaction. "The whole Judean countryside and all the people of Jerusalem went out to him" (Mark 1:5).

SPEAKING TO THE CRISIS

Yet there was sorrow as well as joyful expectation in the crowds. These were not naïve religious fools. The world's greatest imperial power utterly dominated their nation. Israel's limited local self-government was corrupt and venal. Think of Kyrgyzstan or Armenia under the Soviet empire. Could such an insignificant, down-trodden nation really be the hope of the world?

Various messiahs appeared from time to time, claiming to be liberators anointed by God. Always the rebels were ruthlessly caught and killed, while Rome clamped down. The Roman historian Josephus tells of one rebellious Egyptian Jew who assembled a crowd of followers just outside Jerusalem on the Mount of Olives. He promised his disciples that the walls of the city would fall down before them. Instead, Roman soldiers cut down thousands of the rebels, while the leader himself escaped and was never heard of again.

There was a great gulf between what Israel was and what they were meant to be, between God's promises of blessing and their experience of repression and poverty and sinfulness. Every day under Roman rule rubbed the wounds raw again. Clearly, many had concluded, God was punishing them.

Yet many continued to believe the prophetic predictions of glory. When John announced the kingdom come, people poured into the countryside. They came from all strata of society—religious leaders, soldiers, government bureaucrats—to a wild landscape devoid of food and lodging. They came to hear John's news and to make a symbolic gesture of repentance "for the forgiveness of sins." Only if God forgave their sins, they believed, could the kingdom of God come.

A STRANGE WAY TO LAUNCH A CAREER

Picture yourself in that scene, among thousands of people camped in the wilderness, short on food, short on shelter, crowded around John. In that dramatic setting Jesus appeared. He came almost anonymously, catching the attention only of John and a few of his followers. Rather than proclaim himself as Messiah and Son of God, Jesus did a very surprising thing. Jesus came forward to be baptized.

John was shocked. He protested that Jesus ought to be baptizing him, not vice versa. Without disagreeing with John's assessment—false humility was not in Jesus' vocabulary—Jesus nevertheless insisted that baptism was the right thing for him. So John relented and performed the deed. In response God tore open the heavens and gave a visible sign—a dove flying down on Jesus—and an audible message: "This is my Son, whom I love; with him I am well pleased" (Matthew 3:17).

That, strangely enough, is how Jesus began his public career. And I do mean "strangely." I doubt anyone in the twenty-first century would write the script that way. Want to launch a major new initiative? Balloons and fireworks, a march or a banquet might be recommended. You might want to give a speech or have a choir sing. But never baptism.

Go to a bookstore and scan all the religious bestsellers offering to revitalize faith. Does a single one devote a chapter to baptism? Do they even mention baptism?

And yet Jesus chose to kick off his campaign this way. It's one of the few events that all four Gospels record. He began his public ministry with an essentially submissive act, receiving John's baptism at the Jordan River as part of the crowd. He didn't identify with John, the fire-breathing prophet whom everyone crowded to hear. He identified with the straggling pilgrims who came for "baptism of repentance for the forgiveness of sins." Essentially he said, "I am one of them."

If we want to follow Jesus' steps in ministry, we have to ask what this meant to Jesus and how we can imitate it.

THE MEANING OF "SIN" FOR JESUS

Even if nobody explained baptism to you, I think you could guess some of its meaning just from watching. Baptism is like a skit done in mime. It mimics a person washing in water and evokes the idea of cleansing from whatever has polluted your life. No wonder many religions practice some form of baptism. And no wonder that at this crisis point, John called Israel to be baptized.

In Jesus' case, however, a problem arises. According to Christian belief, Jesus was sinless. His life was unpolluted. No washing was necessary. No doubt this explains John's reluctance to baptize him. What did Jesus have to repent of? Of what sin was he guilty?

For me, sin has always seemed purely personal and individual—a dirty stain on my soul for which I alone am responsible. As though in a nightmare I find myself without any hiding place, without any friend, exposed in my horrible naked self. I stand completely alone in my sins.

Given that understanding, Jesus' baptism makes no sense. Jesus had no dirty stain on his soul. He could only be going through the motions with John to show his sympathy for those who really had something to be sorry for. This is how Jesus' baptism was sometimes explained to me: Jesus had to go along with the ritual, like somebody sipping 7-Up at a drunken party just to fit in.

Why would Jesus go through such motions? In particular, why would he make such a charade the centerpiece for launching his ministry?

My individualistic understanding of sin, I now see, leaves me looking at baptism through the wrong end of the telescope. Let me try to turn the telescope around.

When first-century Jews heard the word *sin*, they did not immediately think of individual failings. Their Bible told the story of the Israelite people. It featured national sins—such as worshiping the golden calf, complaining about the food on the trip to the Promised Land, rebelling against Moses' leadership or neglecting the worship of God in the temple. Individuals participated in these sins, of course, but the national impact made the sins noteworthy. Israel sinned. Even David's well-documented dalliance with Bathsheba was not strictly an individual failing. David, as king, stood for the whole nation. As champion he had fought for the whole nation against Goliath. As king his glory was the nation's glory. By the same rule, his sin was the nation's sin.

Israel was one big family. They met the world as a unit, with a family reputation to uphold. If one of them behaved shamefully, all felt ashamed.

People came to John because of a family crisis. They repented of Israel's sins. It's not that they didn't see themselves as sinful individuals—they clearly did—but they saw their personal sins wrapped up in the fate of a sinful nation. They could never fulfill their God-given national destiny unless they became a different kind of family. The first step was to confess that need.

THE PEOPLE OF GOD TOGETHER IN SIN

When I lived in Kenya, a friend told me about the rural church he grew up in. It was a fine, strong, godly body of believers, greatly influenced by the 1950s East African Revival. Then came the 1969 Oathing Crisis. A powerful group of politicians orchestrated secret meetings intended to unify the Kikuyu tribe against other Kenyans. At the meetings, members of the tribe took an oath to their ancestors. This was supposed to bind them to the interests of the Kikuyu against other loyalties.

Christians took a very clear stand against such oaths since they invoked ancestral spirits. My friend's church stated very clearly that they would not participate in any such meetings.

Then, in the dead of night, church leaders were rounded up from their homes and forcibly taken to a secret gathering place. My friend, only a teenager, watched while the elders of his church submitted to the oath, one after another. It took surprisingly little pressure, he said. A few blows, a little ridicule, and they all caved in. None even shed blood before yielding. My friend had been confident in his own strength of will, as only young people can be confident. When his turn came, however, he held out for only a short time. They stripped him to his underwear, and he felt vulnerable, ridiculous. He too took the oath.

Afterward, he felt terribly ashamed. He could not look in the church elders' eyes, and he saw that they could not look in his eyes either. They left the meeting in silence and humiliation. When Sunday came, they went to worship as usual. No one mentioned what had happened. They acted as though nothing had occurred.

Years went by. The church went about its business, but joy had disappeared. The elders preached the same message but without the same power. A cloud of failure and sin hung over the congregation.

Finally, after a decade of dullness, someone bravely stood in a service to confess what he had done. Others did the same. The whole church faced up to its failings, publicly confessing their weakness and sin. Then, and only then, did the church regain an effective witness.

This is the kind of repentance John called Israel to show. He was not singling out individual sinners. Rather, he spoke to Israel as a whole. In that, he was just like every prophet who went before him. The prophets never said, "Some of you are headed for trouble. Some of you need to repent." No, the prophets warned all of Israel. As a people they were chosen. As a people they would be judged. As a people they needed to turn around.

Undoubtedly some individuals—Ahab, Jezebel or Manasseh—were worse than others. Undoubtedly some—Ruth, Hosea or Daniel—lived exemplary lives. Did that remove anyone from the judgment? All Israelites shared disgrace because of sin. The whole nation was punished with exile. All suffered. All must repent.

TEAM PLAYERS

Such a group mentality is almost extinct among Western people, but we see its modern survival in athletic teams. In a baseball game I listened to one night last year, the Boston Red Sox held a lead over the Oakland Athletics until the final innings. Then a relief pitcher came into the game for Boston and gave up two scratch hits. The catcher made a crucial error, allowing a passed ball and then throwing the ball into center field. That allowed Oakland to score both the tying and winning runs.

In an interview after the game, the Sox starting pitcher was asked about his performance. He had pitched extremely well, but he seemed to take no joy in it. Only the loss mattered, and the way his team had played in losing. He felt heartsick. If you lose the game, you share in the disappointment and chagrin even if you personally played flawlessly.

After such a game, the manager may well call a team meeting and ask the team to "repent"—to turn away from sloppy play and to dedicate themselves anew to playing as they ought. Every player will join in that repentance, whether or not he individually has something to repent of.

It sometimes happens that a player says to himself, *This isn't my problem.* He may skip the meeting and let it be known he has nothing to do with the team's failings. If he shows such an attitude, he is likely to be shunned by his teammates. If you belong to the team, you identify with the team in its failings as well as its strengths.

Jesus felt the sins of Israel deeply and personally. He understood that Israel had reached a crisis. Therefore Jesus came to John for baptism. He was not repenting his own individual sins, but Israel's. Since he fully identified with the people of Israel, he fully identified with those sins. He knew that his future and Israel's future were one and the same.

I have suggested, and I will document, that Jesus very deliberately started a movement. He did not start it from scratch, however. Jesus adopted and embraced a very ancient movement—that of historic Judaism. He would shape and reshape it for the purposes of God, just as Moses and Samuel and David had done before him. That's what great leaders do.

He began, however, with a full embrace of his people just as they were, sins and all. Jesus did not cause Israel's problems, but he took on her tragedy. He entered into Israel's experience, carrying her load. He would end his life in the same way: bearing the sins of Israel.

3

JOINING PEOPLE
WHO DISAPPOINT YOU

AT FIRST GLANCE IT SEEMS IMPOSSIBLE to bring Jesus' baptism to bear on our lives today. The whole notion of embracing the sins of Israel through baptism seems too strange and far off from the twenty-first century—like practicing a ritual learned from hieroglyphs in King Tut's tomb. We no longer recognize prophets like John, and there no longer exists an Israel that hopes for the kingdom of God.

Notice, though, one thread of continuity that has survived down the two thousand years. That thread is baptism. Though baptism has become a somewhat obscure ritual in many churches, it is still practiced almost universally as the starting point for a new believer. If you want to follow Jesus today, you begin just the way he did: by getting baptized. His first step is your first step.

But Jesus' baptism makes us rethink what we are doing. Jesus was baptized for the sins of God's people, not for his own personal and individual faults. This teaches something quite at odds with the individualistic spirit of our age. The problems that God intends to fix—and which we must repent of—are bigger than ours as individuals.

Jesus' mission is larger than saving three billion individuals from their sins. He intends to redeem heaven and earth and to found a new kingdom that will never end. He calls us to join in.

Baptism is not an individual act. It is the act of an individual identifying with a group. For Jesus that group was God's people Israel. For those of us who follow Jesus' steps in baptism, that group is God's people the church. The needs of the world require a family that is right with God.

This is a special kind of community—a community that identifies with sin. At baptism we join a group that accepts it is lost.

I mean really lost, in a way that continues into the present moment. Christians give a lot of publicity to successful churches and their winning attitudes. But most of their successes amount to something pretty small from God's way of looking at things. Perhaps in some exceptional churches you find people who are a notch better than their neighbors. But a people to save the world? There is no way! We are no Super People. We are too weak, too compromised, too comfortable with our mediocrity. We are too muddled with sin.

In baptism we join this lost group—a group that in America claims to be shocked by immorality but is as prone to divorce as any group in the history of the world. We join a group that follows Jesus but also frequently follows the buck. We join people who say they are disgusted by Hollywood yet show themselves addicted to its entertainment offerings. We are a people who spend more on dog food than on the poor. We show more pride in our military than our missionaries.

I list some sins of America because that is my church, but I believe that everywhere in the world the church is compromised by sin and prone to its own cultural blindness. Think of the traditions we share. When we are baptized we embrace a history that includes virulent anti-Semitism, which stained all the great church fathers—Luther, Calvin, Augustine, Chrysostom. Our people are guilty of the Crusades and the Inquisition, of apartheid in South Africa and in America. We ignored genocide in Buchenwald, in Rwanda and in the Great Plains of the United States. We are very lost. We have always been lost. Up to the minute we are lost.

When we are baptized in Jesus' name we embrace this body, sins and all, because it is Jesus' body and bears his name. At baptism we repent for the forgiveness of sins—these sins of the church, these sins we share in as individuals, these sins that afflict the whole world.

Does this mean I must accept solidarity with every fast-and-loose televangelist? With mean-spirited fundamentalists? With fatuous liberals who repackage the spirit of the age as progressive Christianity? Yes, yes and yes. If they bear the name of Christ, they bear my name. I belong to them and they to me.

It is much the same as family. My brother the welfare deadbeat remains my brother. My sister who got caught in a corporate scandal remains my sister. I do not approve of their failings and I may criticize them severely, but I feel them as though they were my own. And I will not turn my back on my family, no matter how lost. There will be exceptional cases when I cut ties to a particular relative for reasons of personal safety and to foster reformation. Even then he or she remains in my prayers and in my love.

When Jesus stepped up to be baptized by John, accepting the sins of Israel as his own, his Father sent his Holy Spirit. The Father recognized Jesus as his beloved Son, who pleased him. The Father does the same for all those who take the same step. At baptism he adopts us as his beloved children, members of his family and bearers of his Spirit. He will redeem us, and the world through us. At the very moment we accept that we are lost, we are found.

CHURCH CONSUMERISM

If we fail to grasp baptism in the steps of Jesus, we will consider our commitment to Christ as a purely individual matter—"me and Jesus." Then we will think of ourselves as free individuals, bonded to Jesus but not to anybody else. We will therefore look at church just as a consumer looks at competing products.

That was me. I was a church consumer, and proudly so. I had heard good preaching and good music. I knew an excellent Bible study when I came upon it. A certain style of ministry suited me, and I felt good about recognizing it. I knew what fed me.

Then I moved to Kenya. In the busy city of Nairobi during the late 1970s my wife and I could choose from many churches. However, we did not find many "good" churches, according to our standards. We didn't find the preaching challenging. The music wasn't to our taste. Small group Bible studies were scarce. We did find one church we liked, but many other Americans attended there. Since we wanted to experience a thoroughly African church, we decided against it.

We settled for a church far below our hopes and expectations. An African couple invited us to join them in starting an English-language service in an established Swahili-speaking church. We met in a shed made of corrugated tin. I led the singing with my guitar, which I didn't play very well. No matter, the congregation didn't sing very well. We had no regular preacher so had to invite guest speakers from around the city. Sometimes they didn't appear—telephones and bus service were unpredictable—and so occasionally I got pressed into last-minute service to preach.

This was not the church of our dreams. Sometimes we longed for something else. Yet when I evaluated this experience after four years,

I made an important discovery. I had grown more as a Christian there than at any previous church I attended. I wasn't being "fed," but somehow I put on weight.

Why was that so? At the time I didn't know. Now I believe my wife and I inadvertently stumbled into Jesus' steps. Do you think your church is mediocre? Consider what Jesus felt! He came "not . . . to be served, but to serve" (Matthew 20:28).

From that time on, we have looked for a church where we can serve. We aren't on the hunt for a perfect church to meet our needs, but for a church where people are genuine and open to God, and where we can serve.

Churchgoers infected with consumerism understand church not as a gathering of God's people, but as a program offering. Consciously or not, they look for the church that targets their market profile— their musical tastes, their worship style, their age, race and income level.

Perhaps they may find that "perfect" church and experience consumer contentment. Walking in Jesus' steps, however, is quite different. Jesus identified with God's people, particularly in their sin and trouble. When consumers discover sin and trouble, they head for the door.

We all "need" community. We need the warmth of belonging, of mutual support and of a shared identity. In this world of lonely individualism we need community more than ever.

Yet putting it that way seems to present community as one more consumer good we can go shopping for. Jesus did not shop for the best community to join. He took it as a given that his calling involved serving the troubled and broken community he was born into. He was baptized into that community, and he gave his life serving that community because he understood it as chosen by God.

SKIPPING JERUSALEM

Sometimes I like to fantasize what Jesus' life could have been. Why did he need to limit himself to a backward community, immersing himself in their problems? Jesus could have gone looking for a healthier place. He could have skipped the arguments with legalistic Pharisees. Petty squabbles over Sabbath he could pass over altogether. Why put up with such nonsense?

Jesus could have skipped Jerusalem entirely, setting off from Nazareth straight for the big stage. In Athens he could have talked to the philosophers. In Rome he could have met the emperor. Considering Jesus' gifts, would you doubt his success in these arenas? Have you any question that he would have confounded skeptics and won allegiance from the rich and powerful? Jesus might well have become the most influential person in the world, honored and loved in Rome instead of dying unpublicized in a provincial capital, a left-handed compliment tacked over his head. ("King of the Jews," as seen from Rome, is like "Emperor of Scranton.")

In short, Jesus could have skipped being a Jew. In his day Jews didn't produce great artists and scientists. They were a poor people with a reputation for being difficult. Jesus could have been far more successful without their baggage.

Jesus might have been successful without God's people, but he could not have been God's anointed choice. God had chosen Israel, and "God's gifts and his call are irrevocable" (Romans 11:29). Jesus chose to be baptized with sinful Israel. He identified fully with their self-inflicted woes. That meant spending his whole life with Israel when he might have been more appreciated elsewhere. It meant going to Jerusalem—screwed-up, self-righteous Jerusalem. It meant falling into the hands of mean, proud religious leaders. It meant dying unrecognized and unappreciated.

Jesus became the most influential person in the world, but only by way of Jerusalem, "the city that kills the prophets," and only by way of death.

But I am getting ahead of the story. Baptism was Jesus' beginning. It is the beginning for us today. Baptism means joining the church as surely as it meant, for Jesus, joining Israel. To follow Jesus means walking with God's people, Jesus' "body." It means sticking it out through joy and boredom, in prosperity and budget crunches, in joyful worship and sexual scandals. Baptism even means living through bad music and self-important preachers.

Baptism means carrying these joys and woes on your heart. Jesus' disciple Paul, after listing his many physical sufferings, capped them with this: "Besides everything else, I face daily the pressure of my concern for all the churches. Who is weak, and I do not feel weak? Who is led into sin, and I do not inwardly burn?" (2 Corinthians 11:28-29). To be truly baptized into the body of Jesus Christ is to enter a lifetime of daily weakness, to daily burn with the shame of sin— not just your own but the whole church's.

That is what Jesus accepted when he went to John for baptism. Do you think he found it easy to identify with people like us? "O unbelieving and perverse generation," Jesus exclaimed once. "How long shall I stay with you? How long shall I put up with you?" (Matthew 17:17). I'm sure Jesus did not find it easy, but he came to John seeking baptism.

REMEMBERING MY BAPTISM

I wish churches would stress baptism as much as the Bible does. It should not be shunted aside to the occasional special service.

What changed my attitude toward baptism was an advice column on love and sex I wrote for many years in a magazine for teenagers.

Almost every month I got some version of one question: "What difference does a piece of paper make?" If two people love each other and promise to love forever, why do they need an official wedding? Isn't love what counts?

Does the wedding really matter? As any experienced adult can tell you, it does. Private promises made under the moonlight can vanish in the sun. Living together is not the same. That's why most societies have traditionally insisted that lovers make solemn vows before their community and before God. The wedding ceremony has power to seal a commitment.

I have come to think of baptism as the wedding ceremony of faith. Baptism makes abstract ideas like "commitment" very public and practical. Shouldn't churches celebrate baptisms with the same passion they give to weddings?

After the event, baptisms should be remembered, too—not done and forgotten. In my family we celebrate each person's baptism day like a birthday or an anniversary. We try to mark the day, year after year, and remember what it means.

Perhaps the best way we remember baptism, though, is by participating fully in the body of Christ, the church. At baptism we give ourselves to the people of God in all their troubles and sorrows, just as Jesus did. That sets our course for a lifetime.

I used to think of following Jesus' steps as an individual pilgrimage. Jesus was ahead; I followed behind by myself. Now I see that I can't walk alone. I have to stick close to my brothers and sisters. We are a crowd following Jesus—badly. We get off the path. We lose our bearings. Nevertheless, we seek to walk the way Jesus showed. He promises to get us to the destination, even though we are poor followers. He promises to get us there together.

Some pastors, when they baptize, take a handful of the water and

fling it over the congregation. It's their way of reminding people that
each person's baptism belongs to everybody—that we are "all one in
Christ" when we get baptized into Christ. We need that consciousness if we want to walk in Jesus' steps.

TWO MEN

Years ago while writing historical fiction I did extensive research on
the abolitionist movement. Two historical characters stood out to me.
I gulped down so many of their letters and papers that in the end I
felt I knew them. They started out as good friends, working closely
together to end slavery, but they ended their lives in very different positions.

One was Theodore Weld, a great and charismatic figure. Dramatically converted to Christ through the ministry of Charles Finney,
Weld soon joined the tiny, radical Christian minority that opposed
slavery. Weld may have been the most significant man of the movement—a great speaker, author of several influential books, much
loved by his friends. He persuaded thousands to join the cause. Repeatedly he stood up to mobs who wanted to beat or kill him.

But Theodore Weld did not finish well. Initially he thought that a
few years of persuasion would turn America against slavery. When it
didn't happen, he grew disgusted with his fellow Christians and their
compromised faith. He quit attending church, convinced that it was
populated with hypocrites. He could enjoy a more sanctified time of
worship at home with his wife and children, he thought. He soon
dropped out of the antislavery movement as well—that too was full
of flawed people. Ultimately he gave up the cause altogether. Weld
finished his days running a small school for the children of cultured
Bostonians.

Lewis Tappan was a far less impressive man. A successful businessman in New York City, he appeared stiff and stuffy to most people. He made his greatest contributions to the antislavery movement as a bureaucrat behind the scenes. He edited newspapers, organized meetings, wrote letters, raised funds. Like Weld, he experienced great disappointment with his fellow Christians. Churches persisted in racial prejudice, and most cared very little about slavery. Yet to the end of his days Tappan stayed with the church. He was constantly trying to help reform it and grieving over its failings. One of his many organizing projects was the American Missionary Association, which began through his work freeing the Amistad slaves. (The Steven Spielberg movie *Amistad* tells a fictionalized version of this case.) The organization went on to support other antislavery causes, with Tappan the dynamo that made it go.

During and after the Civil War the American Missionary Association led the way in establishing more than three hundred schools for freed slaves. Some became today's preeminent African American colleges, including Fisk and Howard. Almost a hundred years after Tappan those schools would educate some of the most prominent leaders of the Civil Rights movement, including U.N. ambassador Andrew Young and Coretta Scott King, wife of Martin Luther King Jr.

Both Weld and Tappan were baptized Christians. Weld's baptism, however, seems to have been limited to a transaction between himself and God. The church had no part in it, and he abandoned the church when he saw its failings. Weld never understood that Jesus calls us to identify with his people even at their worst—just as Jesus did, and does.

Tappan did not always like the church, and he certainly fought against its racial prejudice—segregated seating, for example, and segregated Communion. Yet Tappan identified himself as part of the church, sins and all. He never lost his sense of mission within that church. He was at work for Christ until his death, always loyally within the fellowship.

To follow in Jesus' steps begins with a baptism that is more than a transaction between you and God. It means identifying with the people of God, just as Jesus did. You have found your family. You may be ashamed of them, but you cannot pretend to belong to some other people. You may disagree with them on many issues, but you disagree as brothers and sisters.

Baptism means discarding your freedom to do whatever you like with your life. You accept an assignment to serve God's people and to serve with them. "Take my yoke upon you," Jesus said, knowing that few people would ever cheerfully put a yoke on their necks.

THE TOXIC CHURCH

I know many people who object strongly to the idea of identifying with the church. Some feel bruised and abused by the church. Others clearly see its many faults and don't want to hear that they must give their lives to such a flawed institution. Christ's yoke they are willing to bear, but not the church's.

Not long ago I received a letter from a man whose pastor had become unbearably authoritarian. He wanted to know whether he was obligated to stay in that congregation, no matter what. I was glad to tell him that nobody is bound to stay under that kind of leadership. They are free to find another congregation.

Another example: I have often talked to families who are long-time members of a church that lacks a strong youth program. When their children are teenagers needing peer support, the church can't provide it. I advise such families to work hard at improving the youth group, but failing that, to find another church. They are not obliged to sacrifice their children out of loyalty to a particular congregation.

If they leave one congregation, though, they ought to find another. A Christian is not bound to a particular place or a particular leader, but he or she is bound body and soul to the visible church of Jesus Christ. And since the visible church is weak and sinful, those committed to it are almost certain to experience struggle and suffering.

Churches can pose many obstacles to faith. Yet I ask: do you want to walk in Jesus' steps? At his baptism he declared his identification with the sinful people whom God had chosen. He never abandoned that commitment, not even when it cost him his life.

Jesus certainly criticized his fellow Jews. His words to the Pharisees were sharp and cutting. He wept over Jerusalem. He rebuked his disciples. Yet he never pulled away from Israel. He never would abandon them. He went to Jerusalem rather than escaping its limitations. He loved Israel. He would die for Israel.

I ask myself: would I die for the church? For the church I know, with all its faults and flaws?

4

JESUS' TEMPTATIONS

IN JESUS' TEMPTATIONS WE FIND THE second great surprise of his career. First was his baptism—who expects God's anointed to be baptized for sin? And second, who anticipates temptations? After a glorious day when God blesses Jesus and announces him as his beloved Son, we look for a crescendo of glory. Surely the great kingdom of the Son will begin.

Instead we meet the devil. Satan is the aggressor, approaching Jesus with vivid, subtle, compelling temptations. God's own Son is not immune.

From this we learn, perhaps to our disappointment, that temptation is normal. Most of us, when we experience torment and temptation, immediately think we have taken a wrong turn and missed God's will. "I don't know how I could even think of that!" we say in dismay. Jesus' steps suggest that we might react differently. Temptation is no failing, but the natural outgrowth of the baptism of the Holy Spirit. What other conclusion could you draw from Matthew, Mark and Luke's unified contention that God's Spirit led Jesus immediately into the wilderness, where he was tempted?

The Gospel accounts let us see how Jesus responded to these attacks. They offer an extraordinary view of the greatest man who ever lived facing satanic temptation of the highest order. These temptations push us to think the way Jesus thought. They give lessons in facing temptation.

They also reveal a deeper dimension to Jesus' story, one that only occasionally surfaces during his life. On the face of it Jesus spends his days dealing with fractious religious leaders, dense disciples, hungry and sick beggars, Romans, Pharisees, family members, friends. The temptations reveal another level of experience. Underneath the dailyness of Jesus' work is a conflict between powers. These powers go by various names: life versus death, heaven versus hell, holiness versus sin. Jesus lived on the front lines of war between these powers. So do we. Through his temptations we glimpse how the war is waged.

A DIFFERENT KIND OF TEMPTATION

How does one tempt Jesus? Familiar entrapments involve alcohol, sex, anxiety and anger. I believe that Wormwood (C. S. Lewis's fictional tempter in *The Screwtape Letters*) would regard these as sound, basic temptations for everyday Christians. Put a bottle in front of them or have a family member fail to clean up a mess, and you can forget about many Christians for the day. So long as they stay glued to a computer downloading porn or keep twitching angrily at their spouse, they won't accomplish much good of any kind. Ordinary temptations knock us out of the life God wants us to live.

We notice right away that Jesus' temptations are of another kind. They do not aim to trip up somebody merely trying to get through his day untarnished. These temptations go after someone with ministry on his mind, someone who wants to participate in leading the people of God toward salvation.

Do such temptations have anything to do with me? So long as I am content to go about my own business (not God's) untroubled by glory, these temptations will never come my way. When I take up Jesus' mission, however, I put myself in range of satanic bombshells.

JESUS' MISSION

The world has never known a more focused person than Jesus. The Italian filmmaker Pier Paolo Pasolini captured this well in his 1964 *The Gospel According to St. Matthew*. Pasolini portrays Jesus striding rapidly several paces ahead of his disciples, shouting words to them over his shoulder. Pasolini's imagination painted the picture—you won't find it exactly that way in the Gospels—but he captured something that the Bible unquestionably portrays. Jesus knew precisely what he wanted to do and where he wanted to go. His disciples could barely keep up.

Through the centuries people have wondered where Jesus got this consciousness. Did he know that he was God from the time he was a boy? When and how did he discover that he was Israel's Messiah?

We cannot answer these questions. We simply do not have enough data about the development of Jesus' self-consciousness. We can say for certain, however, that Jesus knew his mission from the moment of his baptism. Not that God sent down a detailed mission statement. He didn't need to. God's mission statement was well known to every first-century Jew. If you had asked around on the streets of Jerusalem, you could have been told Jesus' mission.

Beginning with Abraham, God had called Israel to receive his blessing. From that blessing they were to bless the whole world:

I will make you into a great nation

and I will bless you;
I will make your name great,
    and you will be a blessing.
I will bless those who bless you,
    and whoever curses you I will curse;
and all peoples on earth
    will be blessed through you. (Genesis 12:2-3)

To be the light of the world was every Jew's mission statement, not just Jesus'. They were supposed to do it together, as a nation. The prophets' sermons are full of the expectation that Israel will become the center of the universe, shedding light on every nation and drawing the world to Jerusalem, the center of peace. Jesus drew on this expectation when he told his disciples, "You are the light of the world" (Matthew 5:14).

Everything Jesus did—every story he told, every beggar he healed, every symbolic deed he enacted, every prayer he uttered—had to do with the mission to participate in God's long-promised kingdom. Jesus took on this national mission at his baptism. Satan determined to stop him.

That's why we can learn from Jesus' battle with Satan. This is not just Jesus' mission. It belongs to all the family of God. And Satan attempts to sideline it just as surely in us as he did in Jesus.

WHERE IS THE FOCUS?

"Now the serpent was more crafty than any of the wild animals the LORD God had made" (Genesis 3:1). Satan's temptations were extraordinarily shrewd. He designed them not to keep Jesus from success at his God-given vocation, but to make sure Jesus succeeded in the wrong way. That has been Satan's strategy ever since, whenever God's people have begun to take their mission seriously. Satan would like us to work with maximum effectiveness at a goal ten degrees off target.

Satan approached Jesus with three helpful suggestions. All three began with the very dangerous word *if*.

"If you are the Son of God, tell this stone to become bread."

"If you will worship me, it will all be yours."

"If you are the Son of God, throw yourself down from here."

"If you are the Son of God" can be read in two ways. It might be a cynical question, meant to cast doubt on Jesus' identity and his mission. "If you are really the Son of God (though I doubt it very much), prove it to me—and to yourself."

Alternatively, it might be Satan's way of goading Jesus. "If you are the Son of God, act like it. Do miracles. Take risks. Demonstrate your power. What—are you afraid to assert yourself?" As Ajith Fernando writes, "He was reminding Jesus of his privileges."

Either way we read the phrase, we end up in the same place. Satan encourages Jesus to think about himself and to assert himself. Whether he doubts Jesus' identity and calling or aggressively asserts his identity and calling, he's pushing Jesus to think all about "me."

The middle temptation goes in the same direction. "If you will worship me, it will all be yours." Not, "The world in all its splendor will be God's," but "yours." In other words, Satan asks Jesus to think about the legacy he can create for himself.

Satan strikes an extremely vulnerable point in human psychology. I know this chink in my own armor all too well. Wherever I have responsibilities, at whatever level of family, work or community involvement, I tend to focus on myself and my personal ambitions. It can be a negative focus: I become consumed with doubts and self-pity. It can be a positive focus: I become obsessed with my powers and possibilities. I can become quite grandiose in my dreams.

Even in writing this book about Jesus, I find it quite easy to focus on my ambitions as a writer, on the admiration bound to come my way as others read my remarkable insights into Jesus. That is classically a satanic temptation.

I have seen a great deal of this weakness in pastors and Christian workers. As a class of people, pastors are as devoted, capable and idealistic as any I know. Yet they can be unsettled by thoughts about themselves and their position. Pastors, in my experience, often float back and forth between grandiosity and paranoia. They dream of presiding over a thriving spiritual kingdom in which everyone loves and honors them. Then, in an instant, they see enemies everywhere in their congregation (or church staff or denominational headquarters).

We are all subject to this, especially when we are at our most idealistic. The subtlest temptations change the subject from "God and his kingdom" to "me and my prerogatives," "me and the support I deserve," "me and my masterful plans" or "me and my enemies." Such are the temptations that Satan brought to Jesus.

Such temptations go far beyond pastors. Every church I know has a cadre of people whose feelings have been hurt. They have pulled back because something offended them. They don't speak to certain people since they clashed three years back. Their offer to lead the Bible study was ignored, and they haven't forgotten. Since the pastor doesn't value their opinions, they're not going to offer them anymore. What do these hurt feelings have in common? They're all about "me." Surely Satan has tempted successfully.

WHERE TO LOOK FOR HELP

Jesus responds to this focus on "me" in a very interesting fashion. He does not argue with Satan, nor does he rise up and assert himself as God's Son, in whom God is pleased. Rather, Jesus takes himself out of the discussion. He deflects Satan's focus on "me" by quoting Scripture.

Quite remarkably, Jesus answers the three temptations with three quotations from the book of Deuteronomy. I doubt that Jesus chose Deuteronomy at random. It seems very likely that Jesus had been meditating on Deuteronomy during his forty days in the wilderness, which would be completely appropriate for someone called to lead Israel to its true destiny. Deuteronomy is Moses' brooding sermon to Israel as they prepared to enter Palestine after forty years in the wilderness. As they enter the land of their dreams, Moses repeatedly calls Israel to remember God. He warns against forgetting God once they experience material prosperity in the new land. As Jesus prepared to lead Israel into the promised kingdom of God, what better help than to review the words of Moses?

In other words, Jesus did more than quote Scripture. He quoted Scripture intelligently. He evidently had studied and memorized and meditated on a specific Scripture to meet the situation he faced. As temptation came, he drew on that Scripture.

That tells us something important about meeting temptation. The response must be formed long before the moment. Jesus' involvement with Scripture, along with his life with his heavenly Father, created a foundation for his choices. He did not grasp the air looking for help when the pressure was on. He drew on what he already had. Jesus was a man formed by Scripture. Anybody who wants to follow his steps should aim to be the same.

When I am tempted I sometimes imagine that I could neutralize temptation by making my brain operate in a certain train of thought: "have faith," "think about Jesus," "feel God's love" or whatever. In truth, mental tricks do not work against temptation—at least not for long. You can only resist temptation using the tools fixed deep in your life: your grounded understanding of what God wants, rooted in Scripture, and your confidence in God's loving-kindness.

When Jesus stood in temptation, he could not (or did not) order Satan to go away. He made no argument with Satan, nor did he protest that Satan merely wanted to hurt and destroy him. He did not take Satan's bait at all. The Scriptures he quoted moved the discussion sideways, to a subject far from the one Satan had raised. Jesus used no tricks and no special spiritual powers. He did nothing but what you or I could do just as well. Jesus hunkered down on the truth as he had learned it by studying the Bible. Satan could not move him off that. Eventually Satan went away.

If anybody could have argued Satan down, it was Jesus. He could have humiliated Satan, exposing his lies through brilliant analysis. He could also have demonstrated his godly power, ordering Satan to cringe before him. Instead, Jesus said almost nothing. Confronted with temptation, he did not try to speak for himself. He let Scripture speak for him.

The first lesson we learn from Jesus is this: know Scripture. Don't think you are smart enough to argue and fight your way through temptation by yourself. Know the Bible, let it saturate your mind, think it through carefully, and God's Word will argue for you. That is the path Jesus followed.

I realize that knowing the Bible is conventional Christian advice. But is it conventional Christian practice?

The way Jesus quoted Scripture suggests that he soaked it in, meditated on it and memorized long passages, drawing out fundamental principles. When he quoted Scripture to the devil, he didn't just match a verse to a temptation. He had in mind the whole story behind the verse. Even Bible-believing, Bible-quoting churches have moved away from learning the Bible in this kind of depth. Many now speak topically, tell moving personal stories and use the Bible to footnote their points.

We need more than that. Jesus relied on Scripture to answer Satan. Can we manage with a weaker defense?

THE FIRST TEMPTATION: THE TYRANNY OF NEED

When I was twelve or thirteen years old I climbed Mount Whitney, the highest point in the continental United States. Woefully inexperienced, my dad and I took very little food with us on a long and exhausting climb, much of it through snow. At the summit I ate what we had: a few dried apricots. I have never forgotten that moment of revelation. Those leathery apricots seemed to radiate tropical sunshine inside my mouth. I thought I was eating food for the gods. For years afterward, I searched vainly for the same brand of apricots. I thought I had tasted an entirely different fruit. I did not realize that hunger had completely transformed my experience of taste. Hunger changes your brain chemistry.

Jesus' first temptation seized on the fact that he was hungry—no small thing. Having fasted for forty days, Jesus was weak with hunger. Satan had an answer to the problem. If Jesus was truly the Son of God, then he could turn a stone into bread, eat and be renewed.

There is nothing obviously wrong in this suggestion. On the contrary, it seems helpful. Hungry people need to eat. As Jesus would show a little later, he could make bread out of nothing. He could feed five thousand people. Why not do so now, for himself? Why not meet his own needs?

Yet Jesus rejected Satan's suggestion with a verse from Deuteronomy. "It is written: 'Man does not live on bread alone, but on every word that comes from the mouth of God'" (Matthew 4:4).

At first glance, this answer seems beside the point. Of course we don't live on bread alone. Bread nevertheless remains a necessity.

There is a deeper story, however, for those who know Scripture well. Jesus was quoting a passage referring to the Israelite march across Sinai. If you look up that passage, you will learn that Israel's hunger was no accident. God caused it. God then satisfied it by feeding them with manna, the miracle bread that appeared on the ground every morning. God did this to teach Israel "that man does not live on bread alone but on every word that comes from the mouth of the LORD" (Deuteronomy 8:3).

In other words, as Israel followed the path out of slavery and toward the Promised Land, both hunger and miraculous food were part of God's plan, teaching them to depend on God. Nothing happened beyond God's control. He would provide both hunger and food in his own way and time.

Jesus recognized how this narrative applied to his situation. The Spirit had led him into the wilderness to fast. Indirectly but certainly it was God's plan for Jesus to be hungry. Likewise, it was in God's plan that food would be provided at the appropriate time, just as it had been for Israel in the wilderness.

Why not turn stones into bread? The answer is simple, though penetrating: it was not God's time for the fast to end. Scripture said to live "on every word that comes from the mouth of God." Thus Jesus was listening for the Father's words, and it wasn't time to eat.

As Jesus later said, explaining his entire ministry: "I do nothing on my own but speak just what the Father has taught me. The one who sent me is with me; he has not left me alone, for I always do what pleases him" (John 8:28-29). In teaching his disciples, Jesus would pass on this profound challenge. "Do not worry about your life, what you will eat or drink; or about your body, what you will wear. Is not life more important than food, and the body more important than clothes? Look at the birds of the air; they do not sow or reap or store away in barns, and yet your heavenly Father feeds them. Are you not much more valuable than they? . . . Seek first his kingdom and his righteousness, and all these things will be given to you as well" (Matthew 6:25-26, 33).

We must listen to what comes from God's mouth. Jesus knew that and lived that. So he was hungry for a little longer. He had to wait for food, and nobody told him when he would get it.

WHEN YOU GET THE TICKET

I love a story Corrie ten Boom tells in *The Hiding Place*. As a young girl she grew very frightened of death. How could she bear it if her father were to die? Would God give her strength? It was unimaginable. Her father, in answer to her fears, asked about their train trips together. When did he give her the ticket, he asked, that enabled her to ride? Did he give it long in advance? No, she answered, he put it in her hand just as they got on the train—at the moment she needed it.

Her Father in heaven would do the same, said Corrie's father.

This is the philosophy Jesus quietly insists on in the first temptation. Those who live by it—who can wait for God's direction even when life seems desperate—can be accused of foolishness. Aren't they indulging in fatalism, waiting for God and not taking initiative? That would be an accurate assessment if there were no God. But in point of fact, God takes care of his children. They can afford to wait for him.

Often enough, of course, God's Word calls us to take initiative. The kingdom of God is full of risk-taking, as Jesus' career would show. The question is, on whose initiative do we take risks? Do we get direction from God or from our own appetites? Are we directed by dreams of glory, hopes of admiration or fears of humiliation? Or do we listen for God's voice?

I was in my twenties when I went to Kenya. My job was to help start a magazine. I loved the work, utterly challenging and exotic. After an extensive feasibility study, we produced our first issue of *Step*. I walked around Nairobi, admiring the magazine's cover as it gleamed from many newsstands.

After about six months, however, the thrill faded and worries began to grow. Sales were slower than anticipated. We had expected to run a deficit at first, but I began to see that the deficit wouldn't automatically disappear. If something didn't pick up, we would run out of money. All my hard work would be for nothing. My fellow employees would have to find other jobs—no easy thing in East Africa. I would go home to the United States dragging my failure behind me. I would be humiliated. As this very real possibility came home to me, I became quite anxious.

Unlike Jesus, I had no miracle powers. I couldn't command sales to increase, turning stones into readers. I had other powers, though. I could berate people for their failings. I could complain about the nation where I was a guest. I could drive the staff to work harder. I could make an impassioned emergency appeal for more money from supporters at home.

Instead I learned to pray. I began to rely on prayer like breathing, just to get through the day. It was quite possibly my most important and beneficial experience, because it taught me (though I have had to learn the same lesson again, many times) to be still and let God be God.

Sales did pick up and *Step* did succeed, much to my relief. I'm glad it did, and I hope the magazine served God's cause. I don't think success was ever guaranteed, however. In Scripture I see no assurance that our good intentions will be blessed with triumph simply because we are the right kind of spiritual people praying in the right way. Scripture says we live by God's every word. *His* good intentions will be blessed with triumph. Our job is to listen, to wait and to follow. That's what Jesus did when he faced hunger. We don't even know how he was eventually fed. We only know that he did not starve.

At the end of Jesus' life, the same temptation presented itself again. He was arrested. One of his followers pulled out a weapon and hacked at the nearest enemy. Jesus told him to put the sword away. "Do you think I cannot call on my Father, and he will at once put at my disposal more than twelve legions of angels? But how then would the Scriptures be fulfilled that say it must happen in this way?" (Matthew 26:53-54). Jesus had the resources to rescue himself. He did not use them. Instead he listened to God's Word, even though it meant his humiliation and death.

In Suspicion of Activism

This point if taken alone might make us leery of all activism. It might turn us into people who sit around critiquing all efforts to organize and solve problems. Some suspicion of activism is probably a good thing—especially in activistic America. It must be balanced, however, by another important word: obedience. Jesus' scriptural word was hardly negative. "Man does not live on bread alone, but on every word that comes from the mouth of God." Living by God's Word means obeying God's Word. Doesn't Scripture clearly tell us—to mention just one theme—to care for orphans and widows? With millions of orphans and widows due to AIDS, we have plenty to do.

Jesus' life clearly witnessed to the reality of listening to God's direction. The daily discernment of God's will, listening to him as he speaks through Word and Spirit, is one way in which we follow Jesus' steps. He will tell us what to do, if we listen.

We do what he tells us—just that. No crying needs, no sense that the world around us expects certain behavior, no desire to make a mark can substitute for the Word of God. Unless we listen carefully and wait until we hear direction, we will be sidetracked by other agendas—our own or others peoples'—and miss our mission.

THE SECOND TEMPTATION: CUTTING CORNERS TO ACHIEVE GOOD

A second time (using Luke's chronology) Satan offered his help. This time he started from Jesus' mission, as the Word of God had established it. God had called Israel to be the glory and splendor of the nations of the world. Isaiah had seen it this way:

This is what the Sovereign LORD says:

"See, I will beckon to the Gentiles,
I will lift up my banner to the peoples;
they will bring your sons in their arms
and carry your daughters on their shoulders.
Kings will be your foster fathers,
and their queens your nursing mothers.
They will bow down before you with their faces to the ground;
they will lick the dust at your feet.
Then you will know that I am the LORD;
those who hope in me will not be disappointed."
    (Isaiah 49:22-23)

Satan took Jesus onto a high mountain where he could see from one end of the earth to the other. Satan offered just what Isaiah had promised: the authority and splendor of all the nations. Understand, this was a wonderful offer. It was exactly what Jesus was baptized for.

It was entirely God's will. God himself had promised it. Satan said he could get it for Jesus immediately.

Interestingly, Jesus did not dispute Satan's right to make the offer. Would Satan have been able to deliver? Had Jesus accepted the help, would the splendor of the world have withered and darkened while they watched? I suspect so but I do not know for sure. Jesus focused on a different point: the matter of worship.

Satan had a condition: "If you worship me." Notice that he did not say, "Worship me instead of God." Satan is not a monotheist. Either-or is not his way of putting things. Polytheism, he asserts, is a delicious possibility. "You can worship me and him at the same time. We are not in conflict."

In response Jesus quoted Deuteronomy 6:13: "Worship the Lord your God and serve him only" (Luke 4:8). Jesus was a monotheist to the very core.

Jesus might have quoted Old Testament warnings against idolatry and the worship of other gods. Instead, the command Jesus quotes speaks positively. If the first temptation prompts us to listen to God alone, the second tells us to worship God alone. Jesus does not react with a rulebook mentality, warning against improper religion. Instead he leans into that which calls our hearts: true worship, dedicated in complete purity to the one worthy God.

In recent times the word *worship* has become synonymous with a certain kind of singing. That mentality is far too limiting. Genuine worship demands our whole mind, body and soul. Music is certainly a primary way to worship, since it unites our bodies, emotions and thoughts. But worship is also prayer. Worship is service. Worship is confession. Worship is listening to God's Word and responding from the heart. Worship involves consciously putting ourselves in the right attitude before God by "kneeling before him" or "lifting holy hands," a physical, emotional and mental symbol of willing service.

We have a choice every day whether or not to worship God. It requires intentional, disciplined activity. We worship individually in dedicated times as well as throughout the day through prayer, song, posture, reading, meditating, listening. At least once a week we gather in the company of others to do it corporately. Then worship can hit its stride, for it is naturally something we do in company as we encourage and stimulate each other.

Worship is for God only. We do not worship our feelings, our tuneful music, our skillfully led liturgy, our powerful preaching, our impressive, well-dressed congregation. We do not worship our success. We do not worship our plans. Our attention goes to God alone. In his awesome presence, worshiping anything else seems plain stupid.

CUTTING CORNERS

Idealistic, mission-driven people can feel the temptation to compromise. I sometimes try to imagine Satan's offer posed to the president of an organization fighting world hunger. "Today, at a stroke, we can provide a proper diet to all the millions of languishing, hungry people in the world. You know their helpless faces, but you will see them glow with strength and health. Will you bow before someone or something that is not quite worthy of worship in order to achieve this unthinkable good?"

Bob Pierce was undoubtedly one of the most passionate, brilliant men of the postwar generation. Those who knew him loved and admired him. He had dedicated his life to Jesus, and he set no bounds on how far he would go to serve him. As a traveling evangelist he visited Asia repeatedly, beginning in 1947. War had destroyed the economy, and people were starving. Pierce's heart went out to the children. Dragging a movie camera from city to city, he made films to show in America. He launched what would become one of the largest and most effective relief and development organizations in the world, World Vision.

Pierce's extraordinary compassion kept him constantly on the road, with little time left for his family. "I've made an agreement with God," Pierce said, "that I'll take care of His helpless little lambs overseas if He'll take care of mine at home." His daughter Marilee wrote a poignant memoir describing the deprivation of growing up with a famous absent father. One daughter committed suicide after unsuccessfully reaching out to her father for help. Pierce's marriage ended in a legal separation. In a fit of temper against a board that tried to govern his compassionate impulses, Pierce quit World Vision. He became bitter and plagued with severe depression.

Jesus' words might have saved him: "Worship the Lord your God and serve him only." Pierce saw a gleaming vision of love and compassion. He thought God's kingdom had to be accomplished immediately. He cut corners with his family and with his temper. While great good was accomplished, the gleaming vision turned dark before him.

This temptation to cut corners does not apply only to famous public figures. It affects anybody who wants to do good and would like to hurry up the process. People seeking building permits for good causes experience this temptation. So do people wanting to bring morality to the public arena. Those who wish to share Jesus' love with their neighbors may be tempted too. Temptations entice us to shade the truth or to withhold the less pleasant aspects of it. Temptations urge us to use unfair influence, to assault the character of those who oppose us, or simply to indulge righteous anger. We can build up our own reputation, or that of a leader, in a way that is unseemly.

The only cure for such temptations is this: worship the Lord, him only. Actively bend your life to him. We will find it very hard to cut corners while we do that.

We need to help each other. I can't help thinking that plenty of people saw Bob Pierce's dangerous patterns. I know that some of them tried to convince him to change. Others, though, let him off the hook. More than that, they promoted him, quoted him and held him up for admiration. He was an admirable person, but now regret inevitably tinges his memory.

THE THIRD TEMPTATION: TESTING GOD'S LOVE

In his third temptation, Satan quotes Scripture. Perhaps he does so mockingly, as though to say to Jesus, don't think spouting Bible verses will save you.

He chooses verses from Psalm 91, a prayer-poem full of God's love and protection for his people. Here is the passage Satan used:

> He will command his angels concerning you
>   to guard you in all your ways;
> they will lift you up in their hands,
>   so that you will not strike your foot against a stone.
>   (Psalm 91:11-12)

I assume that Jesus could easily have carried along to the next verses:

> You will tread upon the lion and the cobra;
>   you will trample the great lion and the serpent.
> "Because he loves me," says the LORD, "I will rescue him;
>   I will protect him, for he acknowledges my name."
>   (Psalm 91:13-14)

The entire psalm speaks of God's wonderful and unqualified protection for his servant. "No harm will befall you, no disaster will come near your tent" (Psalm 91:10).

Satan has taken Jesus up onto a high temple wall and is urging him to jump. If he is really the Son of God, God will surely protect him as he promised in Scripture. Surely the verses of Psalm 91 apply to Jesus. Why not claim them, Satan asks him. Why not throw yourself off this high place and let the angels rescue you?

What Jesus stands to gain from such a stunt is unclear. Will the miracle make a PR splash? Will it jump-start his attempt to bring God's kingdom to life? Alternatively, will such a miracle overcome any of Jesus' own lingering questions and reassure him once and for all that God is fully on his side? Whatever the point of the demonstration, Jesus does not argue it. Nor does he question Satan's interpretation of Scripture. Instead he quotes Deuteronomy 6:16. "Do not put the Lord your God to the test" (Luke 4:12).

There is a story behind this simple verse, and I am sure Jesus has it in mind. The full quote in Deuteronomy is, "Do not test the LORD your God as you did at Massah." Massah was an arid spot where the Israelites, on their journey to the Promised Land, complained that God had not provided water. They complained so bitterly and persistently that God had Moses strike the rock with his staff, making water gush out.

They witnessed a miracle! Hallelujah! No doubt the Israelites held a celebration service, thanking God for the answer to their prayers.

Yet Psalm 95 comments that God was angry with them for forty years after that—a whole generation. Evidently God does not always like to do miracles.

In Scripture, Massah doesn't refer to the place where God did an outstanding miracle. It stands for the place where Israel went off track. Perhaps the most important comment on the incident comes in the final summary statement in Exodus. Massah is described as the place where "the Israelites quarreled and . . . tested the LORD saying, 'Is the LORD among us or not?'" (Exodus 17:7).

WHERE IS GOD?

Is God here or not? Does God care or not? Does God have power or not? I can sympathize with the Israelites. They were thirsty! They had followed God's call into a wilderness. The empty, arid spaces must have seemed to threaten their lives.

"Is the Lord among us or not?" The question will come to everyone who sets out to follow God, because God is not obvious nor does he work with the kind of predictability we would prefer. C. S. Lewis captured this in his description of Aslan, the lion who represents Christ in the Narnia tales. Aslan appears only at the times he chooses—never at anyone's bidding. When he does appear he is not always as comforting as one might wish. "He'll be coming and going," Mr. Beaver famously said. "One day you'll see him and another you won't. He doesn't like being tied down. . . . He's wild, you know. Not like a tame lion."

A God who cannot be found when you need him is less than perfectly satisfactory. I recall one night during college when I felt simply desperate for some sign that God was real. I walked for miles, looking up into the inky sky and crying out for tangible proof: a flash of light, an audible voice, anything.

I think that's a natural reaction, as natural as craving water in the desert. Yet a natural reaction can lead to an ultimatum: show me a sign or else I quit.

In Jesus' third temptation, Satan proposes a plan to test God's support. Ask God for a miracle, Satan says. In fact, force God's hand by putting yourself into a position where God has to do a miracle. If you are God's Son, God will have to bail you out.

In some circles this might pass for miracle faith—but not in Jesus' circle. Who is he to test God, as though God were a faulty battery? This plan did not come from God, and God never endorsed it. The plan treats God as though he were a mechanical part, guaranteed to perform.

For some years I belonged to a Christian group that had a considerable history of taking risks for God. All through the organization you could hear stories, told with a shake-your-head pride, of evangelists who had launched into the unknown, trusting God to provide. One man felt called to preach the gospel in China, but he had no money to get there. What to do? He bought a one-way ticket to Hawaii, which was all he could afford. When he reached Honolulu, he found a way to the Philippines. From there, God provided a plane ride to China, where he had a wonderful time of ministry.

The group took that as its ideal. If you wanted to hold a rally, you rented an auditorium. God would provide the money to pay. You could hire staff, rent offices, plan events, invite speakers and musicians, do almost anything bold and brash for the gospel. God would provide.

In fact, God often did provide. The stories about miracle faith were intoxicating. The group developed a habit of relying on last-minute miracles. They loved the adrenaline rush that came from daring approaches and eleventh-hour rescues. They believed sincerely that they were relying on God. They were not so quick to admit that they relied equally on kindly donors who wouldn't let well-meaning, enthusiastic young Christians founder.

Eventually those donors tired of bailing out rash plans. So did the evangelists' families—for all too often children and spouses were left to rely on miracles as well. Family breakdowns and financial meltdowns happened frequently. Miracle faith had an addictive quality.

Maybe it was faith. To me it seems more like Massah. Or the faith
that Satan urged on Jesus: jump, and God will have to catch you.

"Do not put the Lord your God to the test." Ultimatums, fleeces,
time limits—they may pose as earnest exercises in prayer, but they
are often fueled by ego, not faith. "God, if you are real, heal my
mother of cancer." Such a prayer may be an earnest plea for God to
help a beloved parent. Very subtly, however, it may become a test of
whether God is willing to perform in the way we demand. We set the
test and expect God to meet it. That puts us in control of God rather
than the other way around.

The group I belonged to has slowly and painfully weaned itself
from reckless plans. Other groups, however, have taken up the approach. The "positive confession" movement advocates faith that
states as true something you want to be true. You say that your
mother is healed, or that your whole community has turned to
Christ. God honors your faith by making it so. Like jumping off the
temple, this can be an attempt to force God's hand.

Ajith Fernando points out that the events at Massah suggest God
"may let us have some things that we demand from him in the wrong
way." He refers to Christians in his poverty-stricken home of Sri
Lanka who crave material security. "When I see some of our choice
Christian leaders leaving Sri Lanka, testifying to 'God's marvelous
provision of a visa and a job,' I really wonder if these could merely be
cases God permitted, similar to his letting the Israelites have the water they demanded in Massah." Fernando notes that some leaders
have ended up economically prosperous but "painfully aware that
they are missing the satisfaction of using their gifts where these are
most needed."

Quite often I meet someone who has bitterly rejected Christian faith because of a deep disappointment. Despite heartfelt prayers, God failed to heal or to provide work for an unemployed husband or to bring back an erring child. The embittered person feels that God has broken faith. He has failed to help in time of need.

Judging by this third temptation, Satan enjoys this way of thinking. He wants people to make ultimatums to God. He knows that even if God answers the prayer—as he did at Massah—one ultimatum will lead to another. Human beings quickly grow addicted to giving God orders.

"God, you have got to . . ." Any time we pray those words, we make ourselves masters and God the servant. Any time we rush ahead expecting God to pick up the pieces, we put God to the test. Any time we make up "tests" for God to pass, we set the agenda for God.

Jesus did not operate that way. Jesus, God's beloved Son, would not put God to the test. He would not jump from the temple to see God work.

And so Satan left him—left him still in the wilderness, without food, without glory, without proof. "He was with the wild animals, and angels attended him" (Mark 1:13).

YOU CAN'T ESCAPE TEMPTATION

Temptation is a central reality of the Christian life. Jesus experienced it, and so will all who follow him. Undoubtedly that's why Jesus told his followers about his experience in the wilderness. (He must have done so. Nobody else was there except Satan.)

Jesus' temptations show that even the best man gets tempted. The temptations also offer us hope: tempters do not always win.

Some people believe that temptation gets to everybody sooner or later. "I'm only human," they say, as though it were axiomatic that human beings fall. Jesus shows us another possibility. He used no supernatural weapons to escape temptation. At his moment of hunger and vulnerability, no miracles came. Jesus did only what lies in the power of every one of his followers.

He attended to God's Word. He worked to burn Scripture into his mind. He thought about Deuteronomy so much that he could quote it to counter Satan's helpful suggestions. God's Word was his food and drink, his source of sustenance.

Jesus would not cut corners. Satan offered a shortcut to glory, but Jesus simply refused. "Worship the Lord your God and serve him only" had worked its way deep into his mind.

Jesus waited for God's timing. He would not force the pace by setting God's agenda for him. Satan tempted Jesus to act so boldly that God would have to come to the rescue. Jesus refused.

Listen to God, worship God, wait for God. Does that sound like the way to change the course of history? Frankly, it does not. Most heavy hitters, religious or otherwise, are known for seizing opportunity, for taking risks, for seeking glory. Perhaps Satan has been teaching leadership development courses.

Jesus' approach sidesteps Satan's suggestions and defers to God. His approach to changing the world is radically God-centered, as we shall see.

5

JESUS' MESSAGE—AND OURS

IN THE KITCHEN OF MY LOCAL GOSPEL mission, which feeds, houses and helps the homeless, I saw a slogan attributed to St. Francis of Assisi. Posted on a bulletin board, the slogan read, "Always preach the gospel, using words if necessary."

I liked this slogan from the moment I saw it. I appreciate people who live out their faith and don't necessarily talk about it. I am biased in favor of Christians who volunteer at the soup kitchen, tutor children and work with the neighborhood conservation committee. They "preach the gospel" through their actions, I am firmly convinced. So I liked the slogan.

Pondering it, though, I began to have second thoughts. "Using words if necessary" makes verbal preaching a second-best choice. I can't make that match up with Jesus' career.

Jesus was well known for serving people. Every single day he helped the poor, the disabled and the socially outcast. His ability to heal sick people and expel their demons drew the large crowds that followed him. Yet words were at the heart of his approach to a needy world.

Matthew begins his account of Jesus' ministry this way: "From that time on Jesus began to preach" (Matthew 4:17). Mark says, "After John was put in prison, Jesus went into Galilee, proclaiming the good news of God" (Mark 1:14). Luke puts it, "Jesus returned to Galilee in the power of the Spirit, and news about him spread through the whole countryside. He taught in their synagogues, and everyone praised him" (Luke 4:14-15).

He taught in the synagogues, and he taught in the open air. Synagogues were community institutions designed to keep faith alive through the study of the Scriptures. Under great pressure from aggressive Greek and Roman culture, Jews found refuge and strength in their synagogues.

Jesus went to the synagogues even though he faced skeptical opposition there. He was a rabbi. Through his baptism he had identified fully with Israel. He had to teach in the synagogues, where Jews would go to hear the Word of God.

Yet he also preached in the open air. Jesus undoubtedly faced less scrutiny from rabbinical critics while preaching from a boat or on a hill. He also attracted a wider audience there—more the sort who would feel uncomfortable at the synagogue.

Regardless of the audience, the basic summary of Jesus' "good news" stayed remarkably consistent. John had preached the same message: "Repent" (which means "turn in a new direction"), "for the kingdom of God is near." Jesus repeated this message in towns and villages throughout Israel. He said much more, but quite consistently he started with this core communication. Through preaching it, he set out to change the world.

As Jesus' followers, we ought to major on preaching too. The trouble is, the words Jesus used—"Repent, for the kingdom of God is near"—were cryptic to all but Jews in Jesus' time, and they remain

cryptic to most people today. If I went door to door with this message, it wouldn't communicate. As a result Christians today have
abandoned any mention of the kingdom of God in reaching out. We
use a variety of slogans or short summaries for our core message,
none of which makes a direct connection to Jesus' preaching.

"You need Jesus."

"Invite Jesus into your heart."

"Admit you are sorry for your sins, and accept that Jesus died to
forgive you."

The "Four Spiritual Laws" is probably the best-known short account of the gospel used during the last fifty years. Its opening line
has shaped evangelistic appeals for an entire generation: "God loves
you and has a wonderful plan for your life."

None of these modern messages mentions the kingdom of God. I
daresay that if you asked the average Christian today to explain the
kingdom of God, you would get a rather confused answer. Yet if we
say we follow Jesus, we really ought to be able to make the connection. If we are part of his movement, then our message should follow
his. That's not to say we must repeat Jesus' message word for word.
He spoke in a particular time and place, and ours is different. Surely,
though, we ought to be able to trace a line from his message to ours.

A NARROW AUDIENCE

Jesus addressed Jews, and he framed his message in terms that only
made sense to Jews. The Gospels tell us that he healed or helped a
handful of Gentiles, but they relate an evangelistic appeal with only
one Samaritan woman in John 4—and she had the advantage of
knowing much of "the story so far" through her Samaritan tradition.

Even if they knew the story behind Jesus' message, Gentiles could
not have felt its full urgency. It was not their story. I remember on

April 24, 1980, hearing the news that an attempt to rescue American hostages in Iran had gone wrong. I was living in Kenya then, and Kenyans were becoming some of my closest friends. But when I heard about the failed rescue, the distance between us struck me forcibly. I felt shamed, humiliated and angry on behalf of my country. My Kenyan friends felt concerned and regretful, but from their perspective the eight deaths were the equivalent of one bad road accident—little more.

That is how even a very sympathetic Gentile would have reacted to Jesus' news about the kingdom. The kingdom was a story that had been building to a climax for two thousand years. But what was this story to Gentiles? Who on earth was Abraham, they might ask, and why should I care? And David, who had been dead for a thousand years—what was he compared to Caesar Augustus? And if little Israel really did get a king again, what difference would that make? The Jews were nobodies—an absolutely second-rate power from an outsider's perspective.

I belabor this point because in order to follow in Jesus' steps we need to fully understand that Jesus did not address our generation. He did not address the whole world. His words and actions eventually affected the whole world, but they were originally tailored to a specific time and place. He spoke to a narrow group, an audience uniquely prepared to understand.

Every Jew who listened to Jesus knew the story and felt it deeply. When Jesus said that all the promises of God—and the promise of Israel—were finally coming true, they responded from the heart. God's rule on earth was reaching its long-expected fulfillment at last. That's why the message is described in shorthand as the "good news." Jesus was announcing incredible eucatastrophe (Tolkien's word for the opposite of a catastrophe). "Everything is coming to a head," he was saying. "God is coming to reign and to bless," he almost shouted to the Jewish nation. "Get up and get ready!"

THE TURNING POINT OF HISTORY

Jesus' message told of a particular event on the horizon. It was like telling Davy Crockett at the Alamo, "Help is on the way." The point was not to make Crockett feel better or to inspire subsequent generations of Texans, but to convey to Crockett important, time-sensitive factual information. The message was falsifiable. Either help would come as announced or it would not. This was not an inspirational message that we can lift from its context and apply to our own.

Jesus said that help was on the way for Israel. Twenty-five years later Paul saw the announcement from a different angle: past tense. Writing to the Corinthians about Old Testament events, he said, "These things . . . were written down as warnings for us, *on whom the fulfillment of the ages has come*" (1 Corinthians 10:11, emphasis added). Jesus announced that the fulfillment of the ages was arriving; Paul reported that it had come. The train had been announced; now it was in the station. By Paul's time, the verdict was in. Jesus had correctly foreseen the greatest turning point in history. What's more, he had brought it in himself. Within that twenty-five-year interval, the kingdom had come.

True enough, the climax of history was not visible in the way most Jews had expected. Many looked for a military liberation. Jesus brought something else—something that has made a far greater impact on world history than any military conquest or political transformation. But one needed "eyes to see" what Jesus had done.

Paul and other first-generation Christians believed God's promises of liberation for Israel had come true. Paul wrote that God "rescued us from the dominion of darkness and brought us into the kingdom of the Son he loves" (Colossians 1:13). Early Christians believed that this liberation had been extended to Gentiles as well as Jews—though this took them some time to understand and required a new vocabulary to explain.

We need to understand that Jesus' preaching targeted one time and place because this keeps us from a very great mistake. Many have tried to see Jesus as a great religious teacher and to understand his message as what N. T. Wright calls "timeless truths." Timeless truths are statements like "God is love," or "You should love your neighbor as yourself." Jesus did make such statements, brilliantly summing up what was taught in the Old Testament. But his mission was not to brilliantly sum up the Old Testament. His unique message was not timeless at all. When he said, "The kingdom of God is at hand," he meant, "It's beginning." Jesus' message is about history—God's action in time and space. As Wright says, "The whole point of it was that Israel's dream was coming true right now."

THE TRICKY THING ABOUT TIME

What does all this have to do with us two thousand years later? Allow me an analogy. On December 17, 1903, Orville and Wilbur Wright announced that they had flown the first airplane. That was news—one-time-only news of a historical breakthrough. Today when an airline announces its scheduled flights from London to New York, it offers news too—the continuation and extension of what the Wright brothers began. The Wrights' message was limited to one time and one place. It was the beginning of something utterly new—often predicted, often dreamed, but never before consummated. It was world-changing. The airline schedule applies that change to the lives of those who need to get to New York from London. It will have to be worked out again and again as air travel and passenger needs change. Next year's schedule will be different from this year's, but both demonstrate the same fundamental truth: you can get there from here by air.

In principle, air travel began when the Wrights made that first flight. Historians use the date to mark the beginning of a new era. However, years went by before the general public got any benefit from the Wrights' achievement. The announcement of flight was exciting, but the practical outworking of that first flight took generations and in fact still continues. Air travel grows and extends and changes. Twenty years from now it will surely be different from what it is today.

Similarly, when Jesus announced, "the kingdom is at hand," he declared the beginning of God's final authority on earth. That was great good news, happening in his time and in his time only. Jesus brought in a new era. He began something unstoppable. It has been growing and developing ever since.

Or take another analogy. In 1865 word spread throughout the world that the Union states had won the American Civil War. The implications were momentous: henceforth all Americans were free citizens. That propositional truth about the dignity of all Americans became real through a historical event. Its implications have been unfolding ever since—for example, in the civil rights movement almost a hundred years later. In fact, we are not yet done unfolding those implications as we consider such diverse issues as abortion and gay rights, which raise questions about who has status as a citizen and what rights citizenship implies.

PREACHING IN JESUS' STEPS

If we want to follow Jesus' steps, we have to talk about an event. Call it the Jesus event. Jesus' life was the turning point in the history of

Israel, in the history of the world and in the history of every human being.

If we say a timeless truth such as, "God loves you and has a wonderful plan for your life," the logical response is, "What makes you think so?" The only good answer is to tell the story of what God has done, continues to do and plans to do. The story of Jesus is the best evidence for the assertion that God loves you and has a wonderful plan for your life.

That story stands behind all our modern-day slogans:

"You need Jesus."

"Invite Jesus into your heart."

"Admit you're sorry for your sins and accept that Jesus died to forgive you."

"God loves you and has a wonderful plan for your life."

When we understand the Jesus event, these slogans no longer float in the eternal present of religious consciousness. They lose their mystical, me-centered spiritual associations and gain a factual clarity. They are rooted in historical events, in an amazing leader, in an ancient family story, in a social movement that under Jesus' direction has grown to be as large and deeply rooted as any in history. When we preach the gospel, we announce what God has done to change the world. We offer our conviction that God is transforming the world and that each of us can take part in the transformation.

THE MAN IN THE BUBBLE

The "Four Spiritual Laws" account, which begins by stating, "God loves you and has a wonderful plan for your life," finishes with two line drawings. In each drawing a circle represents your life. Inside the circle is a throne, the "seat of authority" in your life. In one circle—the "before Christ" life—the self sits on the throne, while Jesus waits outside the circle. In the second circle, Christ has come inside to sit on the throne, displacing the self.

I have used this diagram in talking to nonbelievers, and I know firsthand that it effectively communicates the surrender of personal autonomy to Jesus. The problem comes when we try to turn the diagram into the heart of the gospel. For the diagram is a perfect sketch of individualism. The man in the bubble floats alone, detached from history, culture, friends or church. Do the bubbles ever get together? Do they ever go anywhere? Do they have a history? Do they have a purpose? Not in this story. Only inside the bubble does any change occur. It is a universe of its own.

Furthermore, change comes only at the direction of the self inside the bubble. He is the decisive figure, the man of power. God's power and his plans for the universe hardly figure. There is no kingdom of God—or if there is, it extends only as far as the bubble extends.

The "Four Spiritual Laws," taken together, give a broader perspective. They tell about the problems of humankind separated from God by sin and the decisive intervention of Jesus Christ through his death and resurrection. (The booklet attempts to portray these historical events as immutable "laws," but nonetheless a gospel story comes through.)

As a very simplified outline, the "Four Spiritual Laws" introduces the gospel. Its ending place, however—the self in the bubble— reveals how narrowly we have understood the problem. Salvation is not for individuals inside their personal bubbles. Salvation is for everything. All of creation must be redeemed. Society must be redeemed. Families must be redeemed. Governments must be redeemed. In Jesus, God came to save the world. He is saving the world. "For God did not send his Son into the world to condemn the world, but to save the world through him" (John 3:17).

In the words of Revelation, "The kingdom of the world has become the kingdom of our Lord and of his Christ" (Revelation 11:15). This historical breakthrough began in Palestine and from there reached into the Gentile world, to the heart of the great Roman Empire. It is reaching even to the heart of the postmodern twenty-first century.

Of course, these earth-shaking events make an impact on individual lives. People grasp Jesus' salvation very personally. They see God meeting their needs, whether for healing or for emotional wholeness or for a way to make peace with their neighbors. Live under God's gracious government and you will experience a washing away of sin, an invasion of joy, an awareness of God's power. These are not mere psychological quirks benefiting those with a taste for religion. They represent real powers of God at work everywhere in the world and freely available to those who recognize and welcome his kingdom. They are powers progressively unfolding in the world. One day everyone will know them.

Here is one slogan to introduce the good news: "Jesus is changing the world. Come and see." The kingdom of God has come on earth. It can be witnessed in time and space. You can find it wherever the people of God gather to worship and do God's work.

6

THE KINGDOM
OF THE IMPROBABLE

JESUS PREACHED TO JEWS, WHO WERE the only ones likely to understand his message. Indeed, all the first Christians were Jewish, and only after considerable struggle did they grasp that others from outside their ethnic heritage could take part in their movement.

Today we see the opposite. Jewish Christians struggle to assert the possibility of following Jesus while remaining Jewish. The vast majority of Christians around the world have no link to their Jewish heritage apart from reading the Bible. Christianity went from a Jewish sect to a worldwide religion lacking any particular ethnic or cultural identity.

Did Jesus intend this transition? Some people say his prophetic ministry to Israel got hijacked and turned into something quite unrelated to Jesus' purposes. (The apostle Paul has often been accused of this.)

Yet Jesus went out of his way—indeed, he offended people—to emphasize that the kingdom of God was not for Jews alone. Jesus had a far wider, more inclusive idea. Luke records a fascinating encounter

Jesus had in his hometown of Nazareth early in his career. Jesus went to his home synagogue and taught there, first by reading a passage from Isaiah and then by teaching that "today" Isaiah's prophecy was "fulfilled in your hearing" (Luke 4:21). Here are the words that Jesus read:

> The Spirit of the Lord is on me,
>> because he has anointed me
>> to preach good news to the poor.
> He has sent me to proclaim freedom for the prisoners
>> and recovery of sight for the blind,
> to release the oppressed,
>> to proclaim the year of the Lord's favor. (Luke 4:18-19)

A traditional interpretation sees these words as describing various facets of Jesus' ministry. He healed blind people. He spoke good news to the poor. Taking the prophecy quite literally, Christian groups have used these verses to justify their "kingdom ministries" (1) to the poor, (2) to prisoners, (3) to the blind and (4) to those oppressed by unjust governments or economic forces.

They are right in a very general sense. In the new era of the kingdom that Jesus announced, all kinds of ministry to needy people are justified. The kingdom of God brings justice, health and peace—and these may come through ministries to the poor, to the blind, to prisoners and to the oppressed, among others.

In a literal sense, though, this traditional interpretation misses Jesus' clear meaning, which his audience understood perfectly. There is a reason why this story is included in Luke, and it has nothing to do with ministries to poor people, blind people or prisoners.

If you read the passage from Isaiah in its original context, you will find that it clearly refers to God's promise to restore Israel from exile

in Babylon. Isaiah goes on, "They will rebuild the ancient ruins. . . . /
They will renew the ruined cities / that have been devastated for generations. . . . / You will feed on the wealth of nations, / and in their
riches you will boast. / Instead of their shame, / my people will receive a double portion. . . . / In my faithfulness I will reward them /
and make an everlasting covenant with them" (Isaiah 61:4-8).

Anybody who studies Isaiah—and I am sure Jesus did—will recognize what is going on in these predictions. Isaiah spoke to Israel
about a specific historical reality: her destruction by Babylon. After
that war most of Israel's population was deported, her cities razed
and farmland allowed to go to seed. In a deliberate insult to Israel's
religion, Babylon knocked down the temple and burned it. Isaiah in-
terprets this in a strange way, not as a victory of pagan forces over Israel's God, but as God's own victory. All this happened, he says, as a
punishment from God because of Israel's sins.

Yet Isaiah also predicts repeatedly that God will forgive, that Israel
will return to her land, that the cities will be rebuilt and that a period
of great blessing will begin. That is the sense of the passage Jesus
read.

In that passage, "the poor," "the oppressed," "the prisoners" and
"the blind" all refer to the same people. They are the people of Israel,
taken as prisoners to Babylon, blind to God's love for them, oppressed by their captivity and their own sinfulness.

Since Jesus says these prisoners are liberated at the very moment
he speaks, he implicitly maintains that Israel has remained captive,
blind, poor and oppressed, even though they returned physically
from Babylon five hundred years before. The audience listening to
Jesus—his former neighbors—is poor, blind and imprisoned, according to Jesus. The exile has continued to Jesus' own day. Sins still
dominate their national reality. God has not forgiven and restored

them. However, Jesus has good news as well. At this exact moment, in their hearing, their long-predicted liberation has come. God is forgiving their sins and returning to bless them.

No wonder that "all spoke well of him" (Luke 4:22).

Certainly the town's excitement did not come from the thought that Jesus was launching a ministry outreach to the blind. Their excitement stemmed from the possibility that their nation would be liberated, rebuilt and reconsecrated. That longed-for event was what Jesus came home to announce. He had been saying precisely the same thing in his core message: the kingdom of God is at hand.

Religious Nationalism

In the warm bath of his neighbors' approval, however, Jesus went on to something new. He went on to offend them. He brought into the conversation the great prophets Elijah and Elisha, Israelite heroes, but he described their ministries in terms that Nazareth seems not to have heard before. Jesus pointed out that during a time of great suffering in Israel, God sent Elijah right past the door of starving Israelite widows to care for and live with a Gentile widow. Similarly, God allowed many lepers in Israel to suffer but sent Elisha to heal the military general of an enemy nation.

To judge by past experience, Jesus suggested, the blessings of God's kingdom might not turn out the way people expect.

These comments so incensed Jesus' former neighbors that they turned into an angry mob right in the synagogue and tried to kill him. I used to have a hard time believing this scene. I found such instant, murderous fury hard to conceive. In recent years, though, I have found it making sense. Maybe that is because the murderous fury of our world has come closer to home since September 11, 2001.

A little creative use of the imagination illuminates what happened at Nazareth. Imagine a similar scene in Palestine today. Suppose an imam, preaching in a present-day Palestinian mosque, announces that he has a vision for the fulfillment of Palestinian dreams for a homeland. Suppose he shows through his reading of the Koran that this plan will begin with Allah showing his favor and blessing to the Israelis. How would his audience like that? Such an imam might get himself killed.

You can change the characters how you wish: imagine Jesus as a yeshiva student preaching in an Orthodox settler synagogue, saying that the God of Abraham wants to pour out his blessing on Palestinians. Make him a Serbian Orthodox priest who blesses the local Muslims. Make him a Sri Lankan Buddhist monk proclaiming that the Tamil Tigers represent the Buddha's spirit better than his own Sinhalese community. Make him a fundamentalist preacher telling his congregation that God is blessing gay activists and liberals instead of them. Where ethnic and religious hostility grow sufficiently intense, such an upside-down sermon may provoke anger and even mob violence, just as it did for Jesus.

RELIGIOUS INTOLERANCE

To understand Jesus' preaching, you have to scrub away any image of the Holy Land as a dusty, calm locale where Jesus harped on love to gatherings of peaceful peasants. Palestine was perhaps as calm then as it is today. Its people were oppressed and many were angry. Some were ready to kill—and some did kill. Cultural and religious differences were intense. Jews considered Gentiles as morally vicious. You might as well throw pearls among pigs as talk to them about God. The dislike and disdain were reciprocated. Romans viewed Jews something like the way many Westerners view Arabs today: as incompetent religious fanatics, endlessly quarrelsome. The Roman occupation was brutally efficient and efficiently brutal. Jews hated it. Riot and insurrection always danced in the shadows when Jesus spoke of the coming of the kingdom of God.

The violent world of first-century Palestine seems distant from the suburban America where I live. Yet I cannot think of an environment more relevant to the larger world surrounding my sunny suburb. Religious and ethnic intolerance, violence held in esteem—these are hardly out of date.

Jesus, who preached almost exclusively to Jews, would not say what his side wanted to hear. He pressed them to see that God would reach beyond them, as the Bible had always said. Further, he took seriously the Old Testament warnings that ethnic Israel might miss the good news altogether. Jesus preached almost exclusively to Jews, but he spoke at Nazareth of God's great care for non-Jews.

Jesus brought incredibly good news and extraordinarily volatile news. The kingdom was not a matter of individual piety but of regime change. It would separate families, he warned, and lead his followers to be persecuted and killed. This part of his message is verifiably true: families were broken apart and his followers were killed. Before he was done (and he is not done) millions would die because of what he said. Yet he is called the Prince of Peace. Think of the peace plans in the Middle East and you have some idea of the violence that comes with peace that reaches across to the enemy.

Jesus knew a God whose agenda disturbs our hometown comfort. As God told Jonah, so Jesus told Nazareth: I love the people you hate.

THE BEATITUDES

In both Matthew and Luke, Jesus' first extended talk begins with what are usually called the Beatitudes.

Blessed are the poor in spirit,
>   for theirs is the kingdom of heaven.
Blessed are those who mourn,
>   for they will be comforted.
Blessed are the meek,
>   for they will inherit the earth.
Blessed are those who hunger and thirst for righteousness,
>   for they will be filled.
Blessed are the merciful,
>   for they will be shown mercy.
Blessed are the pure in heart,
>   for they will see God.
Blessed are the peacemakers,
>   for they will be called sons of God.
Blessed are those who are persecuted because of righteousness,
>   for theirs is the kingdom of heaven. (Matthew 5:3-10)

Luke's version is shorter and pithier:

Blessed are you who are poor,
>   for yours is the kingdom of God.
Blessed are you who hunger now,
>   for you will be satisfied.
Blessed are you who weep now,
>   for you will laugh.
Blessed are you when men hate you,
>   when they exclude you and insult you
>   and reject your name as evil, because of the Son of Man.

Rejoice in that day and leap for joy, because great is your reward in heaven. (Luke 6:20-23)

If you read just the second part of each line—the results of these blessings—you get a good general description of the fulfillment of God's promises to Israel. Once again, Jesus announces the long-awaited "kingdom of God."

- God's people experience the blessing of living under God's government.
- God's people are comforted and filled.
- God's people take charge of the earth.
- God's people are forgiven.
- God's people see God.
- God's people are recognized as his children.

The Beatitudes paint a beautiful vision of people living in God's presence, under his rule, filled and fed and forgiven. Jesus said nothing original or controversial here. The prophets had been promising this to Israelites for generations.

Originality and controversy come with Jesus' assertion that this is all coming true right now. He is not talking about blessings someday and to some hypothetical people. He doesn't say, "Blessed you can be." He says, "Blessed are." This is a historical announcement. These people get the benefits of God's kingdom.

Several theories were circulating among Jews about how to achieve such "kingdom of God" results. The Pharisees thought God would bless Israel if they obeyed the law more carefully. That's why they pestered Jesus about washing his hands and keeping the Sabbath. The Qumran community thought Israelites should go into the desert to set up monastic communities. The Zealots favored a guerilla war against the oppressors. These groups, and perhaps others as well, all believed that they knew how to bring in God's kingdom—or at least how to keep from obstructing it.

Jesus opposed all three theories. He fiercely disagreed with the Pharisaic interpretation of the law, he was no monk, and he preached peace, not war.

I grew up reading the Beatitudes (wrongly, I now think) as an alternative approach to getting God to release his blessings. Jesus' followers, according to this interpretation, should strive to be poor in spirit, meek, hungry for righteousness, pure in heart and so on. They would get God's blessings through such spiritual attitudes. (This interpretation works better for the sermon in Matthew than for the one reported in Luke. How could Jesus tell needy people to strive for poverty, hunger, misery and hatred?)

I no longer think that Jesus was giving moral directions in the Beatitudes. I think he was announcing further details of the kingdom. He had already announced that the time had come for the kingdom to break into the open. Now he was announcing who would be blessed by it. To carry on with the analogy of the Wright brothers, he had announced the first airplane. Now he was telling who got to fly.

THE POOR IN SPIRIT COME TO JESUS

It happened—as Dallas Willard helpfully points out—that all around Jesus were plenty of examples of the kind of people Jesus had in mind.

> News about him spread all over Syria, and people brought to him all who were ill with various diseases, those suffering severe pain, the demon-possessed, those having seizures, and the paralyzed, and he healed them. Large crowds from Galilee, the Decapolis, Jerusalem, Judea and the region across the Jordan followed him.

Now when he saw the crowds, he went up on a mountainside and sat down. His disciples came to him, and he began to teach them, saying:

"Blessed are the poor in spirit . . . " (Matthew 4:24-5:3)

One imagines him gesturing to the sick, bedraggled, desperate people on all sides. Their eyes gleam with hope and anguish. They are sick, and the medical profession can do nothing. They long to live in a just regime where they can make a decent living instead of having tax collectors arbitrarily confiscate their property. Some are hungry, living hand to mouth, day to day. At the synagogue they hear the Scriptures read, promising God's peace and prosperity and justice. They can taste it like a thirsty man can taste water. Jesus announces that people like them—beaten down in spirit, miserable, lacking in confidence, hungering for justice—are to be blessed as the kingdom comes in. (The blessings have already begun. Hasn't he healed many?)

Jesus extends the announcement to good-hearted people who seem to have no weight in the world: the merciful, the pure in heart, the peacemakers, people who live by God's standard and only suffer for it. Such people seem ineffective and powerless—twigs in the flood of historical events. Yet these people, too, God is blessing as his kingdom breaks in. (As Luke's version adds, others will find not blessing but curses: the rich, the well fed, those who are always laughing, those whom everyone admires. Many of these will see nothing but grief in the new kingdom. Think of the rich young ruler, of Caiaphas, of Pilate, who stand so high above the merciful, the peacemakers, the pure in heart.)

In the Beatitudes Jesus announces the great paradox he will stress so often in his ministry: that the last are being brought to the head of the line. In the words of Jesus' mother (who perhaps sang this song to him when he was a baby):

> He has brought down rulers from their thrones
> > but has lifted up the humble.
> He has filled the hungry with good things
> > but has sent the rich away empty.
> He has helped his servant Israel,
> > remembering to be merciful
> to Abraham and his descendants forever,
> > even as he said to our fathers. (Luke 1:52-55)

God is turning the world upside down.

Jesus never suggested that Israelites could bring on the kingdom of God by being humble, nor even that they could speed up God's work by their good behavior. God's kingdom does not ultimately depend on human agency at all. God's new government comes, Jesus taught in his parables, as secretly as a net slipping through the waters. It grows as surprisingly as a tiny mustard seed. It comes without warning, like a master returning from a long trip. As Jesus had told his neighbors in Nazareth, God's mercy reaches beyond his chosen people to help the sick Syrian enemy and the helpless pagan widow. He blesses the improbable.

The scene was right there before their eyes, if they could see it. Jesus' blessings did not go to the righteous and well fed, generally speaking. They came to ordinary people desperate for hope—poor people, hungry people, sick people, sad people, ostracized people, people who had to forfeit their family's respect to come to Jesus. Throughout his ministry Jesus carried on in this pattern, blessing sinners, tax collectors and lepers.

WHO IS IMPROBABLE TODAY?
The average North American or European Christian is a long way

from that hillside scene where Jesus pronounced the Beatitudes. We are not poor people, nor poor in spirit. We don't know many improbable people to bless. We are too respectable.

If we follow Jesus' steps, however, we will be pulled outward and downward. A gospel that blesses the improbable must be announced to the improbable. What is more, it will appeal to the improbable.

And so it does. The people of God are constantly pulled downward and outward, where they find receptivity. That's why the Salvation Army and World Vision are two of the largest charitable organizations in the world. They are led by Christians who, like Jesus, bless the improbable. That's why every city in the United States has a rescue mission. That's why in soup kitchens or homeless shelters you will find so many Christians serving as volunteers.

That's why the first Jewish Christians, against their will, broke out of ethnic isolation and preached to Gentiles about the Jewish Messiah. That's why Italian missionaries spread the gospel to pagan England, and Irish missionaries to Spain. That's why British missionaries died by the hundreds taking the gospel to India and Africa. That's why American missionaries today are learning Arabic and trying to find ways to befriend Muslims, despite the "clash of civilizations" that should make them enemies.

That's why in the first century the gospel spread so rapidly to Greeks and Romans, people most Jews never considered eligible. That's why the center of the church in turn passed to northern Europe, to people the Romans called barbarians. That's why the churches of the developing world have eclipsed the churches of Europe. The improbables have a history of responding.

Within any particular society, the improbable hear Jesus' call. The poor, the "sinners" and the tax collectors came to Jesus. The weak, the confused, the poorly educated, the emotionally needy—the de-

spised and worthless of a wealthy, knowledge-based society—have a
habit of taking up seats in church.

Jesus announced blessings to the poor. We get to work out the full
meaning of his breakthrough. He lived a restricted life—speaking
only in his own small country and almost exclusively to his own ethnic group. We get to be part of the upside-down world that grew
from those beginnings. We get to do greater things than he did. (As
he predicted we would—see John 14:12.) We get to bless the improbable of the entire world.

We proclaim the breakthrough events of the first century, by
which the world was irreversibly changed. We not only announce
these life-changing events, we ourselves embody their follow-
through. We announce and demonstrate God's rule as it reaches beyond our safe communities to bless the poor and those who count
themselves our enemies.

This is what God is doing. Implicit in Jesus' announcement—to
his neighbors at Nazareth and to his disciples who heard the Sermon
on the Mount—is the question, Will you join? Will you leave the
cozy environment of your own circle of friends, your own ethnic
group, your own social class, your own country, your own people,
and join the kingdom? Will you join God and the people of God in
his persistent love for your enemies and his embrace of the improbables?

BANQUET OF BEGGARS

At a banquet given by a prominent Pharisee, Jesus observed people
vying for the most honored seats as they came to the table. Apparently there was no assigned seating. The host had assumed the guests
knew their status and could sort out the pecking order for themselves. The result, though, was competition and posturing.

In response, Jesus produced a parable. It is an odd parable, sounding more like advice on etiquette than the typical short story Jesus told. Jesus offers practical wisdom to the social strivers. Take the humblest seats, he says, lest someone more important come later and displace you. If you take too high a seat you might get publicly humiliated. If you take a humble place, on the other hand, your host just might come in and move you to a better seat (Luke 14:7-11).

Luke calls this advice a parable. How so? It is a parable because it embroiders on the very well-known Old Testament parable of the banquet. In the Scriptures God prepares a banquet on his holy mountain. It is "a feast of rich food *for all peoples*, a banquet of aged wine—the best of meats and the finest of wines" (Isaiah 25:6, emphasis added). Isaiah offers the banquet as a parable of the kingdom of God, when Israel will come into its own in the ultimate celebration. Of course the Pharisees expect to eat at this banquet. They believe in the resurrection of the dead, when God will bring the whole Jewish family back to life to celebrate God's kingdom.

When Jesus gives etiquette advice for a banquet, he is slyly talking about the final banquet. The Pharisees stand to get this connection: they know the metaphor of the kingdom banquet as well as they know their names. Jesus says to the Pharisees, leave room for others who may come late but receive more honor than you. Remember that the banquet is for all peoples. Don't put yourself too high.

In Luke's telling, Jesus goes on. When you give a banquet, he says, don't invite your friends, relatives or rich neighbors. Instead invite "the poor, the crippled, the lame, the blind, and you will be blessed. Although they cannot repay you, you will be repaid at the resurrection of the righteous" (Luke 14:13-14). In other words, build your community for the resurrection by inviting those who can offer you nothing. Anticipate the resurrection banquet by inviting all peoples now.

Jesus goes on to offer another banquet parable. The master plans a banquet, he says, but his regular guests make excuses why they cannot come. As a result the master sends his servant to scour the countryside for guests, inviting the homeless and disabled—indeed, anybody but the original guests (Luke 14:15-24). God will have a party, Jesus is saying, even if the people he has invited find excuses. God will invite the improbables. He will make them come.

In Jesus' first parable, people are warned to leave room for late-comers at the banquet. In the second parable, they are warned to start living by the inclusiveness that God will show in his final banquet. In the third parable, Jesus warns them not to miss the banquet entirely by making excuses. For God's banquet, the homeless and the disabled—exactly the wrong people—get invited (Luke 14:23).

THE WRONG KIND

If anything is plain in Jesus' life, it's that he welcomed the wrong people. To start a movement he ought to have looked for good people with influence—professionals and theologians and community leaders, among others. Instead, Jesus consistently ate with sinners and tax collectors. Prostitutes wept over him and cleaned his feet with their hair. One of his Twelve he picked up directly from the tax-collecting booth, where only traitors and quislings could be found.

When the Pharisees criticized him for these associations, Jesus made no apology. On the contrary, he implied that the Pharisees were in trouble because they thought themselves too good for such company.

This was Jesus' persistent criticism of his beloved Israel. They had developed a pessimistically separatist outlook on the world. They had become a family that only socialized with family because the neighborhood had become too dangerous. They had become like Christians who attend Christian schools not because they value a Christian education, but because they fear the contamination of non-Christians.

Jesus was an optimist, not in the sense that he thought the world a good and pleasant place, but in that he knew God's influence would work outward, anywhere. It was yeast, spreading through the dough. It was the mustard seed, growing mysteriously from a tiny seed into a great bush.

So Jesus refused to exclude. Rather he pulled people in. Once his disciples told him that they had encountered a man doing ministry in Jesus' name. Since he didn't belong to their party, they tried to stop him. This may be the earliest recorded instance of brand protection. The disciples were asking how to protect the "Jesus" brand, lest it be watered down. Jesus told them not to bother. "Whoever is not against you is for you," he said (Luke 9:50).

Later, on their way to Jerusalem, he sent some disciples into a Samaritan village to make preparation for his arrival. The Samaritans would not welcome him. It seems that they deliberately insulted Jesus' supporters because they were on a pilgrimage to Jerusalem. Refusing hospitality is a serious offense in Middle Eastern society, particularly to religious pilgrims. James and John were ready to "call fire down from heaven" to destroy the village (Luke 9:54).

Jesus rebuked the disciples. He would not pay back evil with evil. An insult from despised enemies of God's people he would simply ignore. He moved on.

Such moves went against survival tactics for Israel. Shouldn't they protect their "brand"—that is, their unique culture and morality? How in the world could a Jew say, "Whoever is not against us is for us"? Yet Jesus did. He did not worry about assimilation or contamination. He felt no need to retaliate against an insult. He believed and practiced that "the one who is in you is greater than the one who is in the world" (1 John 4:4).

SENDING OUR INVITATIONS

The obvious implication is that Jesus' followers should invite the whole world, and especially the poor and degraded. If you look at the composition of the Christian church worldwide, you see that somebody has taken this message seriously. One hundred years ago Christians were mostly white and of European heritage. Today Christians worldwide look like the world, with Africa and Asia leading the parade to the banquet. The glory of the church today is this completely international, multiethnic character.

Christianity started as a Jewish sect, so separated from the world that Peter found it difficult to eat a meal with a non-Jew (Galatians 2:11-13). We have come a long way toward God's banquet, though we still have a long way to go.

We are meant to welcome people who, by everything natural, will never want to come. Expect the Jewish university professor. Invite the Mexican day laborer, the Indian computer programmer, the Saudi Arabian prince. Have we saved a place for them? Do we eagerly look for them to arrive? Are we willing to invest in relationship with them? I think most of us would have to say no, if we are honest. In most cases we're so sure they will say no that we say no for them.

They may, of course, say no for themselves. On another occasion Jesus added a character to his parable of the banquet: a guest who showed up without the proper clothes. The master's tolerance, shown in his invitation of all peoples, did not extend that far. Everyone is invited, but all must dress appropriately. The man who wouldn't dress for the party was thrown out of it (Matthew 22:1-14). Jesus maintained, in short, that standards apply. But they are the Master's standards, not ours. They reflect a change of clothes that anyone can make.

It is true that most churches, being human institutions, tend to reflect a particular culture. Congregations adopt a certain language and style of worship that reflect the members' ethnic and cultural background. In a city like Los Angeles you can find African American congregations, Korean congregations, Chinese congregations, Hispanic congregations, Armenian congregations and Anglo congregations—to name only a few. I see no harm in this. The final banquet is for all peoples, and each must have its own language, culture and style. God made all the ethnicities of the world, and he rejoices in them. His kingdom is more like a salad than a melting pot.

In fact, Jesus did not criticize Israel for being Jewish. He was himself one hundred percent Jewish, and most of his ministry was to other Jews. He understood God's purposes to be worked out through Israel, with all its particularity.

The problem came when Israel built walls rather than bridges, when they failed to see their mission to bless the whole world, when they responded to the assaults of the world with hatred or defensiveness rather than love. So with us. Ethnic-specific congregations are not contrary to God's will, but those congregations need to actively welcome others to the banquet. They need to make space for them. They need to invite them. They need to actively love them.

We live in an incredible day, unprecedented in history, where the immense variety of the peoples of the world is visible and accessible to us. The day of the great banquet no longer seems so far off. We can see the outline of a world in which all peoples—indeed, even all creation (Colossians 1:19-20)—celebrate God's glory together.

We need to know our fellow guests. As a journalist I beat my head against my editors' certainty that Americans aren't interested in any story that comes from outside the United States unless it's about war or disaster. We are going to a party without knowing the first thing about the other guests.

Ignorance shades into ethnic or cultural prejudice. The less we know, the more we fear. Racism and prejudice keep us from welcoming people who are different from us. We need to resolutely confront our own prejudices, and others'. That means finding ways to talk frankly with people who see life differently than we do. Dialogue can be painful and upsetting, but it makes us ready for the banquet.

We also need worship tolerance. It's a fact that worship is deeply cultural. Our music, language, style, imagery and concerns all flow from our God-given culture. There's nothing wrong with that. In fact it's beautiful.

The trouble comes when we're incapable of finding glory in other people's worship. In Anglo America we've been plagued by something shamefully called "worship wars." This isn't even between cultures. It's between generations within a single, homogenous culture. Some older Christians find themselves incapable of listening to younger people's praise music without scorn. Scorn for other people's worship of God! Younger people—who are supposedly enlightened and flexible—may be equally scornful of older Christians' love of (stodgy) hymns and (outdated) organ music. Many people have told me, in all seriousness, that they simply cannot worship in a certain style. They ought to be deeply worried. They must sing with these people eternally!

Worship wars are a minor skirmish within a narrow group of Western society. The attitudes behind the wars, however, afflict us all deeply. Worship intolerance is one factor keeping black and white and Latino and Asian from worshiping together. "People will come from east and west," but we can hardly join them at the table unless we are converted to worship tolerance. If we approach worship as consumers, we will want only what we like. If on the other hand we approach worship as a family reunion, we will seek to learn each other's tunes.

Finally, we need optimism. I see many signs that Christians have the same fearful pessimism that evidently marked the Pharisees. Need we fear Islamists? Secular humanists? Scientists? If we have Jesus' optimism and strength, we will make places at the table for the most unlikely people. The kingdom of God cannot be engulfed by any tide!

What distinguished Jesus was not his cosmopolitan outlook. He was fully and deeply enmeshed in his Jewish culture and time, with its limitations. Jesus knew, however, of a great day dawning, of a better banquet coming, and he made ready. Within his own context he opened himself to improbable people. He ate with the sinner and the tax collector, the people generally despised. Wherever we are, in whatever cultural context, we can do the same. Thus we make ready for the great banquet.

7

PREACHING
FOR A MOVEMENT

FROM THE PERSPECTIVE OF OUR TIME, Jesus related to crowds in a very odd way. He was fantastically popular. Hordes of people packed around him so thick he sometimes could hardly manage ordinary activities like eating, walking or resting. As he traveled from town to town in Galilee, trying to maximize outreach, Jesus always welcomed those who approached him, talking to them, healing their diseases and sometimes even feeding them.

For a modern evangelist (or politician or any public figure) such crowds would set the blood racing. He or she would try to attract as many people as possible, appealing to the masses to "come to Jesus" and to give their lives to his cause. The more the better, and by all means get them to make some commitment. At least get them on the mailing list!

But here is the odd thing: Jesus made no appeal for mass response. Look for an occasion when Jesus had anything like an altar call, and you will look in vain. The closest he came was his appeal in Matthew 11:28-30, when he urged all the weary and burdened to come to him and take on his yoke. His yoke is easy, Jesus said, though it remains a yoke.

More often Jesus warned people off following him. Luke records that he told the crowds, "If anyone comes to me and does not hate his father and mother, his wife and children, his brothers and sisters—yes, even his own life—he cannot be my disciple" (Luke 14:26).

Jesus spread his gospel message to as many people as possible, and yet he typically concluded his teaching with a very uninspiring, "He who has ears, let him hear." That represented a challenge: make sense of this if you can! Jesus had a message that was not for the casual listener. It required effort. It was a nut to crack.

Jesus' parable of the sower says as much. He used it to explain why he spoke in parables so much of the time. The gist of the tale is that a lot of seed goes to waste. Much of the sower's effort seems pointless, multiplying nothing but weeds, withered plants and birds. Yet some seed reaches good soil and produces a great crop. Jesus' story is three parts failure and one part success, but paradoxically it ends in a fabulous harvest.

Jesus clearly did not try to develop a mass following. Popularity he never trusted or encouraged. But neither was he a lonely prophet, crying in the wilderness. Rather, he preached to find good soil: followers who would absorb a deep understanding of how God wanted to rule the world and who would unreservedly join in the work. Jesus did more than declare that God's kingdom was at hand and welcome the improbable to it. He deliberately chose to develop a team of disciples, training them to become leaders in the renewal of Israel. He preached to create a movement. He taught to train disciples. As he told them, "You are the salt of the earth. . . . You are the light of the world" (Matthew 5:13-14).

They would in turn teach others to follow Jesus' way. In his final instructions Jesus explicitly told his followers to carry on training as he had: "Make disciples" (Matthew 28:19). "Train [them] . . . in this way of life. . . . Instruct them in the practice of all I have commanded you" (The Message).

I know of only one group that operates as Jesus did: revolutionaries. Typically they broadcast their message, whether Marxist or Islamist or nationalist. But revolutionaries recruit very carefully. They do not seek legions of untrained, half-committed enthusiasts. They need people who will belong to the cause, heart and soul. They look for trustworthy operatives.

THE WEAKNESS OF FOLLOW-UP

For many years I thought Jesus' command to "make disciples" was fulfilled by "follow-up." Evangelists urged people to "come to Jesus," and "follow-up" tried to ensure that prayers of commitment led to a lasting change of life.

"Follow-up" is added on. In Part A we try to convince a maximum number of people to ask Jesus to forgive their sins and to take charge of their lives. In Part B we urge them to read the Bible, pray and join a church. We give them Bible study materials and try to place them in a fellowship.

Part B sounds like this: "Now that you have bought your new car, you will want to find a good mechanic to consult about maintenance and to ask for help with any mechanical problems." The mechanic is useful, but he is not intrinsically part of owning a new car. Part B follows logically but is quite separate from Part A. That's why automobile dealerships have a sales department and a service department.

Jesus operated differently, however. For Jesus, there was only one part. He preached to the crowds in such a way as to discourage all but the most persistent, those who would "follow up" on their own by listening carefully and asking questions. Only those who persevered in following him and seeking understanding would gain the secrets of the kingdom.

The late John Wimber offered a good example of this approach. The man who taught him about the kingdom in a series of home Bible studies actively discouraged Wimber from making a commitment. As Wimber grew excited by the kingdom message, he wanted to give his life to Jesus. His friend made him wait—to take time to be absolutely sure that he wanted the kingdom with all his heart. Wimber credited that man for preparing him to stick to Jesus through thick and thin.

By contrast, much evangelism tries to make commitment as easy as possible. Pastor Tod Bolsinger, author of *It Takes a Church to Raise a Christian*, recalls his days as a youth evangelist. "I can remember saying to kids, 'There's no church to join, there's nothing to commit to, this is only about a relationship with Jesus.'"

Actually, hardly anything could be less like a relationship with Jesus. He spoke of a narrow way and warned disciples that they had to be willing to carry a cross. When people began to follow Jesus, they joined a band of disciples.

THE MESSAGE OF THE MEDIUM

Jesus had another way of appealing for commitment: he preached as the leader of a team. This made a significant difference in the way people heard him.

Jesus never did anything alone, except pray. Every time he preached, every time he stopped on the road, every time he ate dinner in someone's house, he had his followers along. (His talk with Nicodemus [John 3:1-21] may be an exception, but not necessarily—the record only says that Nicodemus came by night, not that they were alone. It is quite possible that all the disciples were in the room, listening to this astonishing dialogue. That would explain why Jesus used "we" in verse 11.)

Communications guru Marshall McLuhan famously said, "The medium is the message." When Jesus preached, his medium included his traveling band of disciples. The message was, "You can join."

Picture yourself in a Galilean village when Jesus comes to town, preaching and healing the sick. You carefully listen to what he says and watch what he does. If you are attracted, you follow him from market to synagogue, wanting to learn more. Your eyes are on Jesus, but you also can't help noticing the people who accompany him everywhere. They stand out as strangers in town. If you are fascinated by Jesus and want to know more, if you track him from place to place and house to house, you will naturally fall in with these disciples. You will watch them for clues as to what it is like to follow Jesus.

"You can join." Seeing Jesus with his traveling band—ordinary people like you—the next step is to move into their circle. "You can join" means moving with the band. That was the only way to follow up on Jesus—in company with his traveling band.

Evangelism in Jesus' steps is a group project. Perhaps one person does the preaching, but a band of disciples should be close at hand, visibly part of the movement. Success is not when people raise their hands and say they have prayed to accept Jesus. Success is when people join the band and begin to share its life.

TRAINING MATERIALS

If you stayed close to Jesus you would be likely to overhear him training this band. Matthew and Luke describe Jesus teaching the Sermon on the Mount to his disciples, with larger crowds listening over their shoulders (Matthew 5:1; 7:28-29; Luke 6:17-20). The teaching was aimed at the committed few, but it was open information to the masses. From overhearing this, the crowds knew that if they joined Jesus' band they would be expected to live up to these standards.

Recently I was perusing a poster taken from the bestseller titled *Life's Little Instruction Book*. It lists all the good advice that parents wisely give their children, such as, "Say thank you often," "Give at least three compliments every day," and "Always leave the toilet seat in the down position." I happened to be reading the Sermon on the Mount at the time. The contrast struck me forcibly.

> Anyone who is angry with his brother will be subject to judgment. (Matthew 5:22)

> Anyone who looks at a woman lustfully has already committed adultery with her in his heart. If your right eye causes you to sin, gouge it out. (Matthew 5:28-29)

> Simply let your "Yes" be "Yes," and your "No," "No"; anything beyond this comes from the evil one. (Matthew 5:37)

> If someone wants to sue you and take your tunic, let him have your cloak as well. (Matthew 5:40)

> Love your enemies and pray for those who persecute you. (Matthew 5:44)

In comparison to the mundane, conformist wisdom of *Life's Little Instruction Book*, Jesus' words have a powerful and uncompromising majesty. If you are in the little band listening to these words, you will be quite aware that Jesus has the highest expectations. These are not lofty truths about the nature of reality, but practical instructions on what he expects of his disciples. He wants his followers absolutely free from contempt and bitterness, their relationships untainted by lust, their words lacking manipulation and deception. Why? Because they have joined a new community, a renewed Israel, which God will use to transform the world. They are the salt of the earth, the light of the world.

In Matthew's version, Jesus emphasizes that he is not changing a single dotted i in the Old Testament law. He wants to get to the core meaning of the law, having to do with a transformed character and a transformed community. Thus the law against murder fundamentally has to do with eliminating anger and contempt; the law against adultery speaks to lust; regulations about divorce point toward the high value of marriage; regulations about oaths point toward the integrity of a person's speech. Now that God is bringing his kingdom, Jesus' followers must conform to God's deepest intentions.

Some of Jesus' instructions had very direct implications for dealing with the Roman occupation. Jesus told his disciples to love their enemies. He applied that very concretely: bless people when they curse you, pray for people who mistreat you, turn your cheek to those who strike you, give more than demanded to the authorities when they confiscate your only warm clothing (Luke 6:27-36).

These would have been extremely difficult instructions for people chafing under Roman oppression. In one stroke Jesus made it exceedingly clear that God's kingdom would not be built on revolutionary violence. The Maccabees and their imitators the Zealots wanted to fight for God. Jesus was not with them. More importantly, God was not with them. Jesus said God was bringing in a new government, but not through the violence that people expect from a revolutionary movement.

Until Jesus, no one had ever conceived of turning the other cheek as an offensive tactic. No one had suggested defeating Rome by loving the occupying army. Jesus' instructions to his disciples must have seemed amazing and radical. But Jesus was concerned for even bigger problems than Rome. All the powers of evil would be against them. They would conquer these enemies by love.

A lot of energy has been expended trying to decide how these words affect a Christian's involvement with government. Can he or she take up arms as a soldier? As a police officer? Is it even right to work for the government, which functions by coercion?

These are important questions, but perhaps we ought to expend more energy asking what these words imply about a Christian's involvement with the church. Who are the enemies of God's people, and how do we treat them? As a renewed people of God, how do we respond to assaults?

We see enemies within our denominations—wrong-headed factions, dangerous theological trends. We see enemies in our culture—people determined to scrub Christian influence out of the public world. Often we fight with weaponry remarkably similar to that used by secular political factions. If they assault us, we assault them back.

It should not be so. With absolute clarity Jesus told those first disciples how to deal with enemies—enemies who would gladly kill them. Those instructions apply to us—to Jesus' band of disciples—today. Jesus intended to start a movement that would be known for loving its enemies.

THE IRONY OF FIRST-CENTURY EVANGELISM

First-century Christians were extraordinary evangelists. Starting from the most disadvantaged position in society, they brought thousands and ultimately millions of people to faith in Jesus. Yet to judge by the New Testament letters, those first Christians put no emphasis at all on evangelism. None of the Epistles say much about doing it. Paul never urges Christians to look for opportunities to share their faith. Peter says Christians should be prepared to explain their faith if asked (1 Peter 3:15), but he doesn't suggest any outreach.

In modern terms, these churches apparently didn't preach sermons about evangelism and offered no Sunday school classes on how to witness. Nor did they organize campaigns to reach out to their neighbors. Instead, the New Testament epistles pay great attention to how followers should live. Letters encourage Christians to get along with each other, to act in harmony and love and truth within the fellowship. They also seek to be sure that the churches maintain correct doctrine. The emphasis is largely inward: how to grasp their identity as God's people and how to live out that identity.

How, then, were they such an extraordinary missionary church? The reason, I think, is that they spoke Jesus' message from within a functioning, loving community. They represented Jesus' appeal: "Join us!" His good news of the kingdom was visibly at work in their life together. They spoke of Jesus' life and death breaking open a new kingdom, God's kingdom. The door was clearly open for anyone to enter and participate because they welcomed strangers and reached out to the improbable.

WITNESSING TO THE PAGAN WEST

A friend who read this book at an early stage of its development asked at this point, "How do you want us to follow in Jesus' steps? Join the church? You already said that."

Yes, for the individual, "Join the church" is correct advice. That is hardly the end of the story, however. We are so accustomed to individualism that we find it hard to think about collective action. Following Jesus' steps is not just an individual matter. The body of

Christ, together, follows Jesus. The whole community must witness to Jesus' good news that the kingdom has come and demonstrate what it means to live as God's community.

Theologian and missionary Lesslie Newbigin spent most of his life as a missionary to India, but when he retired and returned home to England, he got a terrible shock. The formerly "Christian" nation now showed more resistance to Jesus' gospel than India. When he went door to door in the neighborhood of his church, he found that Indian and Asian immigrants politely welcomed him, while his fellow English were likely to slam the door in his face when they learned he was a pastor. Newbigin spent his remaining years reflecting on how to re-evangelize the tough, cynical culture of the modern West. "How can this strange story of God made man, of a crucified savior, of resurrection and new creation become credible for those whose entire mental training has conditioned them to believe that the real world is the world that can be satisfactorily explained and managed without the hypothesis of God? I know of only one clue to the answering of that question, only one real hermeneutic of the gospel: congregations that believe it."

This does not imply preaching "come to church" as though that were the same as "come to Jesus." The gospel does not present the church as a savior. Rather the church is the place where the Savior lives. The message can be heard, rising out of the church: "Jesus is changing the world. Come and join us as we follow Jesus."

The church is a parade of crippled people helping each other to hobble along. They have grins on their faces. They also have grimaces. Excited to see where Jesus leads, they call out as they go, "Come with us! Walk with us!" God made a decisive intervention in history through the life of Jesus. Something began, real and visible. The church is the beginning of the resurrected world.

That means taking the Sermon on the Mount seriously as it teaches disciples how to live. Do members of our band know these expectations? Do we speak of them with each other?

It also means taking our band out into the wider world, just as Jesus did with his band of disciples. Nobody could accuse Jesus and his disciples of being otherworldly. They paid attention to the needs of the crowds they encountered as they traveled and proclaimed and healed. So it should be today. Where believers work together to engage their cities, neighborhoods, schools, political associations and businesses, they have opportunity to speak of the transformations Jesus makes. When they go out as teams, they show by their lives and relationships how the kingdom of God is growing and what it would be like to join.

As people baptized into God's band, we put ourselves on display. Yes, we are imperfect disciples, but nevertheless we are what it looks like to follow Jesus. If you join the band you become one of us, learning to do the work and to live the life that Jesus taught us to live. "Come and join us as we follow Jesus." Jesus chose his disciples in a way that showed his intention to launch a movement. We are that movement—the very thing that Jesus lived and died to create.

8

THE RADICAL CENTER

JESUS BUILT HIS BAND AROUND TWELVE disciples, whom he called to follow him. Asking people to follow you—literally to follow—is a radical move. Consider how it would seem today if an evangelist came into a city for a week's meetings, picked out some young people and after one or two encounters asked them to leave town with him—to quit school, leave their families and follow. I believe I can predict the reaction. "Take my son with you? I'll call the police!"

Not everyone heard such a call. As far as we know, most of Jesus' followers became attached to him through a process of gradual fascination. Attracted by Jesus, they watched him and listened to him. Eventually they joined his band of followers. Some disciples—the family group of Mary, Martha and Lazarus come to mind—evidently didn't sell their property and travel with Jesus. Perhaps the majority of his followers stayed in their homes, continuing their careers and families and friendships.

For a smaller group—and this is the group the Gospels focus on—Jesus' summons was abrupt and decisive. Often they were going about their business when Jesus interrupted them and called them to be his followers. Jesus simply said, "Follow me." They left everything behind.

Take the calling of Peter, James and John. Luke's account begins with a classic snapshot of Jesus preaching by the Sea of Galilee, with people crowding around (Luke 5:1). Near him some fishermen have completed a night's work and are cleaning their nets. Unlike the gathered crowds, they show no signs of interest in the preacher. They have to earn a living.

Despite their disinterest, Jesus commandeers one of their boats for a pulpit. When he is done speaking, Jesus singles out Peter to take the boat farther out, to cast for fish. I think I can hear Peter's resigned, peevish tone when he says he will do what the rabbi says. Peter can't help making a professional footnote, however: we've been at this all night, without catching anything. Peter knows fishing. Rabbis, he assumes, don't.

No sooner do the nets go in the water than they begin to twitch and pull with a heavy catch. Peter was wrong. Jesus, the amateur, has stumbled on a large school of fish.

Peter has a strange reaction. Instead of being grateful to Jesus for this remarkable catch, he throws himself down before Jesus and asks him to leave. "I am a sinful man!" he says. Jesus brushes this aside and tells him not to be afraid. "From now on you will catch men." Peter and his partners James and John immediately leave their nets and boats to follow Jesus.

TO CATCH THE WORLD

Notice how Jesus majestically appropriates everything for his purpose. First he takes the boat. From the fishermen's perspective the boat is a tool for catching fish, their tool—but Jesus takes it for another purpose, his purpose. Then he commandeers the fishermen, invading their profession. He tells them where to place the boat as they cast their nets. However much they know about catching fish, he knows more. Last but not least, he takes control of their lives. He is not content to let them be godly fishermen. He will transform them into "fishers of men."

The phrase has lost its biting edge. How about "man hunters"? Jesus shows an unbending determination to catch the world. Careers, indeed lives will be taken as tools for his mission.

To these and other disciples, Jesus simply says, "Follow me." His call is absolute. The response is absolute as well. The chosen get up and go, leaving everything behind.

Later, Jesus calls together all his disciples and chooses twelve as "apostles" (Luke 6:13). The number twelve would jump out to a first-century Jewish reader. Twelve was the number of the twelve brothers, the sons of Jacob who created the twelve tribes of Israel. Jesus' choice of twelve hints broadly at what he intends. His chosen twelve are the brothers who will create a renewed Israel. He is starting afresh, reconstituting God's chosen people.

Sometime after the twelve are named, Jesus' mother and brothers arrive to see him. They stand outside the house where he is teaching, asking after him. When he hears they have come, Jesus asks, "Who are my mother and my brothers?" He looks around at his listeners. "Here are my mother and my brothers! Whoever does God's will is my brother and sister and mother" (Mark 3:33-34).

In the Israelite tradition, family is a serious matter. Jesus seems to be discarding tradition and blood in order to build something new.

Jesus warned his disciples that following him would mean becoming a target. "If the head of the house has been called Beelzebub, how much more the members of his household!" (Matthew 10:25). When Jesus said, "Follow me," he was saying, "Be willing to die."

He hardly needed to say it aloud. Anybody in that time and place could have predicted that Jesus and his followers stood an excellent chance of getting killed. As N. T. Wright has pointed out, someone who talked about kingdoms and acted like he thought he was a king tended to have a short life in Roman times—especially if he lived in a contentious borderland where revolution was always on somebody's agenda.

CALLING IN HIS STEPS

Jesus built his following around a core of disciples whom he deliberately chose and called to a radical lifestyle. Should we do the same? Should we call people to sell all their possessions, to leave their families, to make a radical commitment? Some have thought so and tried to impose radical discipleship on all believers. I think that to do so is to confuse our role with Jesus'.

Some years ago I wrote a book with Dave Dravecky, a baseball player who had come back to play in the major leagues after a cancer operation removed a major muscle in his pitching arm. In order to capture the full texture of Dave's life I literally followed "in his steps." I went with him into the locker room before and after games. I met his baseball friends. I got acquainted with his wife and kids. I flew to his boyhood home in Youngstown, Ohio, and had dinner with his parents and other relatives. I saw the house he grew up in and the Little League field where he played as a child. I visited the Cleveland Clinic and had long conversations with the doctor who had operated on his arm. I went to the rehab clinic and talked with the physical therapist who worked with Dave through a grueling rehabilitation.

I did everything I could to walk where Dave had walked and to understand what he had been through. However, I had no illusions that I was Dave Dravecky. I never once imagined that I could pick up a baseball and pitch in the major leagues. I was following in Dave's steps in order to understand him and to learn from him. I was not duplicating him.

Similarly, when we walk in Jesus' steps we are not pretending to be Jesus. Jesus never confused his disciples' role with his. They could certainly do some of the same things he did, and he expected them to. But Jesus did not ask his disciples to shine as he did on the Mount of Transfiguration. They accompanied him to Jerusalem, but he did not ask them to die as the spotless Lamb of God.

Nor did Jesus tell them to call others with his authority. I am not Jesus. I cannot say, "Follow me," any more than I can say, "I am the vine; you are the branches." Whenever Christians get the idea that they have such authority over others' lives—ordering them to quit their work, to leave their families, to go to a certain place and do a certain task as though they spoke with the voice of God—they end up abusing their authority and creating havoc. Only Jesus, the Master, can call and send disciples with such magnificent authority.

BETWEEN YOU AND GOD?

But we dare not make the opposite mistake. Often enough in our individualized society Christians shrug their shoulders and say, "Your calling is strictly between you and God." That is not really true either. God's calling is, properly, between God and all of us. For he calls his people to be part of a family. And our family absolutely needs people who have responded to a call of radical discipleship. We need missionaries and workers who have sacrificed family, career and home—and sometimes life—to follow Jesus' call. Some must leave the family business to become fishers of men. Not everyone is so called, but some must be. Jesus still calls them.

It is popular to say that all of us are called to give our lives fully to

Jesus. The distinction between clergy and layperson, between carpenters and missionaries, between full-time Christian workers and full-time accountants is unimportant, people say: all are called to the ministry.

That is true enough, but it may serve to obscure another truth: God needs clergy, missionaries and full-time Christian workers who have sacrificed all to radical service. He called the twelve, and others, to leave everything. By no means did all the early Christians hear such a radical call, but some did—and it was extremely important that they obey.

If you study great breakthrough periods in church history, you inevitably learn of women and men who heard the same radical call. Antony of Egypt left his life of privilege to go into the desert to pray. He was the founder of the monastic movement that would shape Christian faith for centuries. Augustine was a talented academic who was called, quite against his will, to quit academia and become a church leader. His works, written from the crucible of pastoral ministry, set the direction of Christian thinking for all time. Francis was a rich young nobleman in Italy who heard Jesus' call to sell all and live by alms. His example spurred a remarkable movement that transformed the medieval church.

All these, and many more less famous, heard Jesus' absolute, uncompromising call, which seemed extraordinarily radical to their friends and neighbors. Perhaps they seemed like "fools for Christ," to use Paul's phrase for the apostles (1 Corinthians 4:10). Andrew Walls says that of twenty-seven Church Missionary Society missionaries sent to Sierra Leone before 1820, fifteen died before the end of their first year. It is doubtful whether today's vibrant church in Africa would have grown up without such sacrifices. To choose to go to Africa as a witness, knowing that death is the most likely result, a person must know a call from Jesus.

Certain forces consistently work to discourage such people. The most significant is common sense. Jesus answered such common-sense objections categorically. When he called one man to follow, the man asked first to go bury his father. "Jesus said to him, 'Let the dead bury their own dead, but you go and proclaim the kingdom of God'" (Luke 9:60). Another man wanted to say goodbye to his family—a reasonable request, one would think. "Jesus replied, 'No one who puts his hand to the plow and looks back is fit for service in the kingdom of God'" (Luke 9:62).

We do not make the call. We cannot tell anyone that Jesus wants him or her to go somewhere that death awaits. To forfeit a career, to sell all and give to the poor—it is not for us to put such expectations on another human being. Only Jesus can. We must become a band of disciples that makes space for Jesus' radical calling. We must be people who consider such callings normal. That has to do with the expectations and the ethos, even the organization, of our church fellowship.

MY LOCAL CHURCH

I can give a more recent and quite unspectacular example. The congregation I belong to has been in existence for 150 years. Through all those years the church has tried to be faithful to Jesus. The Bible has been read, God has been worshiped, prayers have been offered. However, the idea that someone might be called to make great sacrifices and take up full-time Christian service was foreign. The longest memories in the church knew of not one pastor, evangelist or missionary who came from within our congregation. Nobody had sacrificed home, career and family to go out on Jesus' mission.

I realize that full-time Christian work may not represent a call from Jesus. A call to radical service can take shape right in your own home and work—and, on the other hand, people often become pastors and missionaries more or less as career moves. Nevertheless, I suspect my church had been thoroughly de-radicalized. Without realizing it, the gospel message had been hemmed in so that in our vision of God's kingdom, no radical callings were needed.

Then, without any warning, God began to change us. Mike and Cathie became Christians through meeting some members of our church. They were invited to attend our services, were attracted by our fellowship and gradually learned what it meant to follow Jesus. They joined us, committing their lives to Jesus. Soon they were active deacons. Mike was a building contractor. He had a big heart and a big truck, and he and Cathie helped many people in need. They were always available when down-and-out people came into the church needing help. They assisted innumerable families with repairs. They showed up on moving day for countless families.

They could have carried on indefinitely as active, loving Christians who carried on the work of God in the world while continuing in their "normal" lives. Evidently, though, God wanted something else from them. At an all-church retreat, Mike stood up during a time of sharing, saying he felt compelled to tell us something. Then he couldn't say it. His emotions took control, and for the longest, most awkward time he could not enunciate a single word. Tears streamed down his face. Adultery? Murder? Larceny? I feared he was going to confess something terrible. But I was not at all prepared for the words he finally choked out.

"God (choke) is calling me (choke) into the ministry."

Nobody had been talking to him about it. None of his family members had ever done it. Our church had no pattern to suggest it to his mind. The idea came from Jesus, not from any of us. Mike and

Cathie ended up quitting the construction business and enlisting with an organization that works with troubled inner-city children. They carried on for the next twenty years.

Their calling set off a series of callings. Others in our church became pastors, missionaries and Christian workers. A kind of calling that had been nonexistent became common. We became a different kind of church.

This week I sat with a young couple headed for Vietnam. They are bright, capable, well educated, with two young children. Five years ago they visited Vietnam on a two-week trip. They heard God's call and have been preparing ever since to go back. They find it hard to leave friends and family, especially when some members disapprove. Financially, they have made great sacrifices. But they grew up in a Christian community where people listened for such callings from Jesus and where the church endorsed such callings and supported them.

Jesus calls people for radical service. He always has and he always will, because the kind of movement he wants depends on such callings. He could not have done it without the Twelve. He needed the likes of Francis and Patrick and Luther, whose lives were wholly and radically devoted to the movement. As the body of Christ we must encourage and support those whom Jesus is calling this way. Are our eyes open, watching to see whom God might call? Are we anxious to encourage, quick to support? Only as we do so can we become, all together, what Jesus calls us to be: the salt of the earth, the light of the world.

I said "all together." There is no doubt that Jesus made a distinction between the core—his twelve disciples, particularly—and the larger group of disciples. It was a distinction without a hierarchy, however. When we see Jesus with Martha and Mary and hear what he says and feels for their brother Lazarus, we know we are not dealing with second-class Christians. They had their role, an important one. We need all kinds to make up Jesus' band.

9

WORKS OF POWER

IN A SMALL, DUSTY MARKET TOWN near Bangalore, India, I was guest preacher at Pastor Jayakanth's Sunday morning service. The church met in an airy, unadorned space defined by a tin roof, plaster walls and concrete floor. Women in brilliant saris sat on mats spread over the floor while men sprawled on plastic chairs in the back. A dense smell of perspiration pervaded the room, a warm scent from mostly poor people who earned their living with their hands. They stood to sing ear-splitting, rhythmic choruses accompanied only by drum and to pray in ecstatic cries. They sat to hear me speak through a translator, listening closely as though sifting my words for a lost coin.

After the service I was besieged with people seeking help. So many crowded around me that I got backed into a corner and couldn't move. My translator told me the request of each person, and I laid hands on their damp heads or held their calloused hands while I prayed. No sooner did I pray for one than another pressed in to take his or her place. Some were sick; some needed work; some wanted husbands to return home. They were oppressed by spirits or worried about upcoming school exams, or they had had family disputes.

Pastor Jayakanth told me that when he arrived in the town seven years before, he found not a single Christian. He was a young engineer with the electric utility, which had transferred him to the area. Though largely untrained as a pastor or an evangelist, he rented a ten-by-ten-foot room and began holding church for anyone who would come. Violent resistance broke out against these meetings, for the town was solidly loyal to its Hindu traditions. On one occasion a large mob dragged Jayakanth to the nearest temple, beating him and threatening to kill him. The breakthrough came after Jayakanth's wife gave premature birth to twins. Doctors said the tiny, underweight children could not survive. Jayakanth prayed and fasted for three days, and the children lived. Suddenly, local people began coming to Jesus. Now Jayakanth counts four hundred baptized Christians, if you include outlying centers where separate meetings are held.

Jayakanth believes in healing prayer. So does his congregation. Jesus' power to heal is close to the heart of their witness. You can hear variations of Jayakanth's story all over the world. Throughout Asia, Africa and South America, where Christians are multiplying fast, you hear of amazing healings done in Jesus' name. People believe in Jesus' power to solve the problems of daily life, and they pray over everything.

JESUS THE HEALER

Jesus would have felt at home in Pastor Jayakanth's church. When the Gospels describe his healing ministry, I am reminded of the scene I faced: crowds of eager people pressing forward, hardly leaving room to breathe. The difference is that for me nothing extraordinary surfaced in answer to my prayers. For Jesus everyone was healed on the spot in a visibly obvious way.

Nobody in our era—not Pastor Jayakanth, not Pentecostal

preacher Benny Hinn, and certainly not me—has experienced healing like the Gospels report about Jesus. To think seriously about following Jesus, we should think about this difference. Are we meant to heal as much as he did? If not, how do we walk in his steps?

Consider some of Matthew's summary statements with their assertion of absolute healing without exception.

People brought to him all who were ill with various diseases . . . and he healed them. (Matthew 4:24)

Many who were demon-possessed were brought to him, and he drove out the spirits with a word and healed all the sick. (Matthew 8:16)

Many followed him, and he healed all their sick. (Matthew 12:15)

When Jesus landed and saw a large crowd, he had compassion on them and healed their sick. (Matthew 14:14)

All who touched him were healed. (Matthew 14:36)

Great crowds came to him, bringing the lame, the blind, the crippled, the mute and many others, and laid them at his feet; and he healed them. (Matthew 15:30)

The Gospels describe in striking detail more than twenty individuals whom Jesus helped. One of my favorite incidents occurred at Peter's home in Capernaum, where Jesus came to visit after synagogue one day. I imagine the household swelling with pride: a new and very popular rabbi has come under the roof. For the women of the house this honor would be particularly meaningful, because in Israelite culture the home was woman's domain, the one place where she could shine.

Worried conversations must have taken place just out of Jesus' hearing, though. Peter's mother-in-law was sick with a high fever. She could not preside over the day, and her sickness undoubtedly distracted the other women. They were pulled in two directions: toward the visiting rabbi and toward care and honor for a sick mother.

"They asked Jesus to help her" (Luke 4:38). Luke does not clarify who "they" are. Perhaps the women of the house whispered to Peter, who passed on the request. Immediately Jesus responded. He "bent over her" and "rebuked the fever." Healed and restored to her position of honor, she got up to wait on the men.

Later, as the sun set, people brought all kinds of sick people to Jesus. He put his hands on each one and healed them. In some cases demons came out, shouting loudly that Jesus was the Son of God—the Messiah. But Jesus rebuked the demons, just as he had rebuked the fever. He would not let them speak (Luke 4:40-41).

Why did Jesus heal? He did it because ordinary people in a village household asked. They needed help and he gave it.

LONG-DISTANCE HEALING

In another Capernaum scene we see Jesus in a public, semi-official role. The village elders approach and ask him to help a local Roman commander, whose "valuable slave" is sick and dying.

Warning signs flash all over this request. The Roman represents everything alien to a Jew. He is an official oppressor who has settled in their town, and he does not belong. He and his house are considered ritually unclean, and a pious Jew would avoid contact with them. Yet the elders urge Jesus to go to his house and heal his slave. They explain that this man is not your usual Roman. He loves Israel and has contributed to the building fund for the synagogue. "This man deserves to have you do this" (Luke 7:4).

Without a word, Jesus sets off. He has probably never before stepped inside a Gentile home. Jesus does not know this man or his "valuable slave," and surely he cannot be terrifically impressed by a contribution to the building fund. Yet he goes. He has been asked to help. He accepts.

Something absolutely unprecedented then occurs. Messengers sent by the Roman official intercept Jesus in the street. Don't come, they say. "For I do not deserve to have you come under my roof. That is why I did not even consider myself worthy to come to you. But say the word, and my servant will be healed" (Luke 7:6-7). When ever has such a thing happened? When ever has a healer been stopped on his way because the person needing help did not feel worthy?

This is indeed a very unusual Roman official. He is genuinely humble and confident that Jesus does not need to do a laying on of hands ritual or to pronounce a blessing in person. Jesus marvels at the man's faith, greater than any he has seen among his fellow Jews. Without ceremony Jesus turns around and heads back. When the Roman's messengers return to the house, they learn that the slave has been healed.

These two healings in the same small city are as unlike as possible: one domestic and one public; one in a family connection, the other to an alien oppressor; one through touch and physical proximity, the other at a distance. It is hard to believe that stories like these were simply invented. They each have the individual detail, the idiosyncrasy of real events.

Every healing story in the Gospels bears that individual stamp. Jesus stops a burial procession to raise an only son back to life. He halts his own procession to heal a trembling woman who has reached out of the pressing crowd to touch him. He throws a legion of demons out of a crazed, naked Gentile man who lives far out of town in the tombs. He raises up a dead girl, the daughter of an important religious official, when people are laughing at him for saying that she is alive. Each scene is different. Jesus never seems to work in the same way twice. Always, though, he accomplishes his goal of healing.

EVEN THE SPIRITS OBEY HIM

Many of Jesus' healings involved removing evil spirits. We tend to think of such exorcisms as quite different from physical healings—frightening and eerie—but in the Gospels they are treated much like any other healing. For example, when John the Baptist sent messengers questioning Jesus' messianic calling, Luke says Jesus "cured many who had diseases, sicknesses and evil spirits" (Luke 7:21). The text reads as though evil spirits were just one variety of illness. Suffering people may present a withered arm to Jesus, or they may present a fever, or they may present evil spirits. Not much is made of the difference.

Jesus was hardly unique in casting out demons. Apparently the Pharisees did it too (Matthew 12:27). Indeed, many people today understand spirits to be responsible for diseases and have experts to root out the spirits. When I lived in Kenya, I was told that the city of Nairobi, skyscrapers and all, had more spirit doctors—*waganga*—than medical doctors. One day my wife, Popie, walking home from the college where she taught, struck up a conversation with a man going in the same direction. She told him that she was a marriage and family counselor. He told her that he was a spirit doctor, on his way to make a house call. Dealing with spirits was his profession. He might as well have been a dentist.

Jesus was not the only one to cast out demons, but he was the only one to show himself complete master of the spirits, commanding them as though they had no choice but to instantly obey. Jesus did no elaborate rituals and used no potions. He carried on almost no conversation with the spirits. He ordered them to come out from their hosts, and invariably they did so, instantly. Jesus said explicitly that this demonstrated God's return to Israel. "If I drive out demons by the finger of God, then the kingdom of God has come to you" (Luke 11:20).

WHAT THE HEALINGS SHOWED

Though a great many people have tried to heal like Jesus, nobody ever has. Surely that is because Jesus uniquely brought in the kingdom of God. God was on the march. He was doing at last what he had said he would do. Israel's history was coming to a climax. The healings were like artillery fire at a battle scene. The bigger the battle, the louder the thunder.

After John the Baptist developed doubts about whether Jesus was really the Messiah, John sent messengers from prison. "Are you the one we have been waiting for?" they asked Jesus. In response Jesus said nothing. He merely carried on healing. After some time he told the messengers, "Go back and report to John what you have seen and heard: The blind receive sight, the lame walk, those who have leprosy are cured, the deaf hear, the dead are raised, and the good news is preached to the poor. Blessed is the man who does not fall away on account of me" (Luke 7:22-23).

Jesus knew that these powerful deeds spoke volumes to John. They demonstrated that God's power was breaking in through Jesus. He was bringing in the long-awaited kingdom.

Jesus' healings demonstrated that he was not talking "spiritually," as though the kingdom would happen in some invisible, inward way. God's kingdom showed itself in the here and now. It affected the natural world in amazing ways.

HOW WE FOLLOW

Jesus' healings made a profound difference in people's lives, much more than the same healings would today. Because of modern medicine and nutrition, most Westerners are healthy most of the time. We confidently expect our children to grow up. We plan for retirement, hardly considering the possibility that we might not live to sixty-five or seventy. Not so in Jesus' era, when perhaps half of all children would die in their first year of life. Lingering illnesses like tuberculosis, malaria and intestinal parasites undoubtedly made a large part of the adult population into the walking dead. Families were extremely vulnerable, for this was mainly a hand-to-mouth society. Losing one working adult to disease could put children at risk of starvation.

Imagine what it was like for those desperate people, crowding thick around Jesus, trying to touch him. They had no clinic. It was Jesus or nothing.

Jesus felt deep compassion. By healing people, he did more than fix their problems. He reinstated them in their rightful place in the community of God's people—the community God had promised to bless. Jesus restored cripples and blind men, who could not join in temple worship because of their disabilities. He touched and healed lepers, who had been ostracized from every human contact. He healed a woman whose menstrual flow of blood rendered her religiously unclean and ruined her possibilities for marriage and family life. He brought children back to life, restoring them to their parents and the circle of family.

These restored individuals were only a beginning of the promises of the kingdom of God. God had promised to restore all of Israel to health (Isaiah 35). A shattered, divided, damaged people was being brought back to family togetherness and shalom. That's why the Gospels often refer to healings and wonders as "signs." They point to something beyond themselves. "The kingdom of God is at hand!"

If healings are signs of the kingdom, I know only one possible response. The answer is not easy for people raised on Western science. As a lifelong Presbyterian, I do not find this comfortable ground. Nevertheless: we have got to be ready to ask God for healing whenever anyone asks. We have got to make room for healing as signs of the kingdom.

Jesus clearly expected his followers to heal. He sent out his twelve apostles to preach and to heal. Later he sent out the seventy-two on the same mission. They came back brimming with excitement. "Even the demons submit to us in your name" (Luke 10:17).

AGAINST NATURE?

Webster's defines the word *miracle* as "an event or effect in the physical world deviating from the laws of nature." I believe most people in the Western world think of miracles this way. God and his supernatural powers stand on one side; the physical laws of the universe stand on the other. A miracle is God's work violating nature. By this way of thinking, a sunrise is not a miracle, however wondrous it may be. If the sun rose in the west one day, that would be a miracle because it violates the natural course of things. A miracle is God doing the impossible and therefore proving his existence as "supernatural."

We think this way about miracles practically as second nature, but I don't believe Jews in the first century thought that way. (Nor do people in many parts of the world today.) The word *miracle* is never used in the New Testament to describe Jesus' amazing deeds. Jesus did "wonders" (*paradoxa*), "acts of power" (*dunameis*), "signs" (*semeia*) or "portents" (*terata*). None of these words lends itself to the God-against-nature distinction. All these words can be applied perfectly well to a sunrise or a storm, which are everyday parts of nature, just as well as to a healing.

Suppose I see a brilliant double rainbow. Science can explain how it occurs. But a rainbow is nonetheless an act of power, a wonder and a sign. Understanding the physics takes away nothing from God's involvement.

For people in the Bible, nature was very close to God. Yahweh had created the universe, and they did not believe he had left it. His voice could be heard in the thunder, his power observed in the storm (Psalm 29). God's acts of power were readily visible in rivers, rainfall, birds and volcanoes (Psalm 104). Heaven was not a far-off place. It was more a hidden dimension to everyday reality, readily accessible through prayer and worship. When God spoke from heaven (as the Bible sometimes mentions him doing) he was actually very near. Ordinarily he was invisible, but he was never inaccessible. He spoke every day, through the sun and the stars, and through his law (Psalm 19). Occasionally, too, he spoke a more particular message, so that prophets could say, "This is what the Lord says." Sometimes he intervened for his people and helped them in an astonishing way, as he did in the Exodus plagues. That was cause for great rejoicing.

Neither special message nor special intervention was contrary to creation, however. The idea would have seemed nonsensical. How could God's activity be contrary to the natural order, since he defined the natural order? The Jews had a larger understanding of the natural order than we typically do. It included God. Creation was not governed by laws. God governed his creation, doing it in such an orderly way that laws could be formulated to describe his rule.

When the Gospel of Mark reports that Jesus at his baptism "saw heaven being torn open and the Spirit descending on him like a dove" (Mark 1:10), Mark does not mean that the laws of the universe were being violated, or that something foreign to nature had occurred. He describes something unusual and significant—a sign, if you will—but not paradigm-shattering. To the contrary, it no more violates the laws of nature than you do when you attend a family reunion. An unusual wholeness is created, a connection made between old friends. God speaks, as he did at the making of the world! This is how creation was designed to be. For heaven is meant to be open to earth, and the Spirit should always descend on God's people.

Jews did not go to Jesus wondering whether he could prove that God existed by doing the impossible. They had another question: would God help his sin-sick people? They knew God could, but would he?

I have never seen what I would call a miracle. That is, I have never seen something occur that was so unusual as to seem impossible. However, I have seen a lot of people get well. I have been sick many times, and I have recovered every time without exception. My mother died of cancer and my dad is dying of Alzheimer's. Yet family love and togetherness provide a sense of God's care in the midst of suffering. Are these not wonders? Signs? Should we not say, "God has come to help his people"? I say it freely, with no sense that I am missing God's blessing because I have not seen the laws of nature broken on my behalf.

I say this glibly, perhaps, because I have not watched a child waste away with cancer, for example. Even should such a heartache come to me, though, I hope I will still thank God for his many blessings—the many healings that take place in a year, even as I regret sorely the one that does not.

How Many Miracles?

God works wonders in the everyday. Jesus' healings, however, were extraordinary. He often helped people in ways that we would call impossible. Withered hands were instantly restored. Lifelong cripples got to their feet and began leaping about. Leprosy victims with rotten and disfigured limbs were suddenly clean and whole. Such events happened frequently around Jesus. No one had ever seen anything like it, and no one has seen anything like it since.

Throughout the Bible you find plenty of similarly amazing wonders, but not in a steady supply. In the times of Moses and Joshua, astonishing miracles happened daily. In the days of David, only a few occurred. When Jeremiah lived, miracles were almost unknown. During Jesus' life, they happened in abundance again. After he left, his disciples also did some amazing wonders, though apparently not to match Jesus'.

God's astonishing works of power are not a constant, like gravity, but an intermittent blessing, like rain. In Jesus' life God sent a downpour.

Today, reports of amazing healings come on the frontiers of witness. Where Christians are few and in danger, where they witness in hostile settings, where people are poor and desperately in need, where people are coming to faith by the thousands, we hear of miracles. Chinese believers, witnessing to Jesus under government persecution, testify to amazing and seemingly impossible wonders. In India, in Africa, in Indonesia, you do not have to go far to find people who came to faith after they witnessed wonderful healings. In other places, however—and not just in the West—extraordinary healings are rare. Do we understand why? I don't think we do. I conclude that signs and wonders are God's business. Our business is to be available.

PARADIGM BREAKDOWN

Some years ago I had a conversation with John Wimber about healing. Wimber was an important church leader in America and Britain during the 1980s. He was best known as the instigator of the "signs and wonders" movement and as founder of the Vineyard denomination of churches. He had a winsome, low-key way that helped spread a charismatic emphasis on healing and other "sign gifts" among younger, well-educated Christians. I interviewed Wimber several times, always finding him thoughtful and stimulating.

Thousands of people swarmed to Wimber's church, largely because they hoped to see a miracle. Reports circulated of wondrous cures and dramatic exorcisms. Wimber himself told amazing stories of wonders God had done. While serving as an adjunct professor at Fuller Seminary, he taught students how to practice ministry marked by "signs and wonders." He fully expected and hoped to see people raised from the dead, he said. Theologians spoke of his ministry setting off a paradigm shift, enabling people to break free from a naturalistic worldview and to incorporate God's power into their everyday dealings. Some people thought Wimber had set the world upside down.

Despite the heady atmosphere, Wimber usually tried to be moderate and irenic with other Christians. In one of my interviews I asked him what he hoped would be the end result of his work as far as the worldwide church was concerned. Did he have in mind to turn the world upside down?

He modestly told me that he only hoped to see churches of all kinds become places where people routinely prayed for physical healing.

After a moment's reflection I told him that I'd never known a church where people didn't routinely pray for physical healing.

It took us a while to understand what the other was saying. Wimber wanted healing prayers to be a public focus. That was how it was done in Vineyard services. At the end of a worship service, the sick or troubled could come to the front of the auditorium and make themselves known. Others would lay hands on them and pray. Sometimes people would shake, tremble, fall on the floor or shout. Whatever God did was on public display.

In the churches I grew up in, people didn't do that. It would have shocked them if someone had suggested it. Yet people certainly prayed for the sick. They just did it in private or in small groups. They avoided publicity and fanfare. Healing was not a public focus of the church, though it might well have been the focus of individuals' prayers (and probably was when someone in the church was seriously ill). Did Presbyterians believe in miracles? Well, yes, in theory, though most would probably say they had never seen one.

Prayers for healing are really not controversial among Christians. Of course we pray when people are in need. How could we not? The key controversy is how public and how publicized those prayers should be—and how expectant people should feel when the prayers are made.

PRAYING IN JESUS' STEPS

In many ways Wimber's approach is closer to Jesus'. Jesus prayed publicly, and he often laid hands on the needy person. He gained a reputation for healing, and people came to him eager for it. He taught his disciples to do it as well. Isn't that how they do it at the Vineyard?

In other respects the Presbyterian approach is closer to Jesus'. Jesus did not want publicity for healings. He healed those who asked for healing, but like a Presbyterian he sought to minimize the fuss and the focus. He never sought publicity. He would just as soon no one knew when he healed. He often told those who benefited to keep it to themselves—to "tell nobody."

I have noted that the Gospels make little distinction between Jesus' healing of diseases and his exorcism of spirits. The spirits' responses do, however, stand out. "Moreover, demons came out of many people, shouting, 'You are the Son of God!'" (Luke 4:41). "What do you want with me, Jesus, Son of the Most High God? I beg you, don't torture me!" (Luke 8:28).

The spirits confirmed verbally what Jesus' great deeds suggested. Spirits involuntarily recognized Jesus as the coming king, with authority over their lives. They identified Jesus as the Messiah, the Son of God. They reacted to his coming kingdom with fear, recognizing that it would be intolerable for them.

Yet, "He would not let the demons speak because they knew who he was" (Mark 1:34).

Wouldn't Jesus want his authority to be widely known? Just the opposite was true. He attempted to hush the remarkable testimony of spirits. He did the same with human beings who had been healed. Apparently he felt that publicity might interfere with his ministry. Perhaps it would have propelled him into public controversy too soon. He wanted to announce the gospel, call disciples and train them in his way of life. Those were his priorities, which pushed the kingdom ahead. Publicity for his healing powers did not.

When skeptics asked him for a sign, Jesus refused to give one (Mark 8:12). He deplored people who wanted to see miracles in order to believe (Matthew 12:39; 16:4). He did not do wonders as an apologetics demonstration.

Jesus was not trying to prove himself or God through miracles. The wonders did authenticate his ministry, but that was not why he did them. He healed and cast out demons and forgave because it was in his nature to do so and in the nature of the kingdom of God.

Wimber believed that praying for healing ought to be second nature. He would say that Christians falter in praying publicly only because their impulse to beg God's help has been suppressed by the materialism and skepticism of our age. With that I fully agree. I thank God for the Pentecostal and charismatic movements because they have served to restore an expectation of God's powerful presence here and now. That is what the kingdom does: it always shows God's authority on earth.

Keeping prayers for healing strictly private and individual, as my Presbyterian heritage taught me to do, blocks the family of God from doing its healing work together. Bringing prayers for healing out into the open keeps people from isolation in their pain. They can be touched, seen, wept over, prayed for in public. And healing can be celebrated in the family.

We should welcome and expect heaven to show itself on earth. That is, after all, what we say in the famous prayer that Jesus taught. "Your kingdom come, your will be done on earth as it is in heaven."

Yet there is a danger in Wimber's approach too. Wimber's book *Power Evangelism* tells Christians to pray for healing in order to show people that God is real. Healing is a means to evangelism, not an end in itself. From there it is a short step to praying for healings in order to stir excitement and gain publicity. That, unfortunately, is what sometimes occurs when publicity and healing prayer run closely together. If we want to walk in Jesus' steps, we will keep our focus on the sick and the needy—not on the publicity that may ensue from our successful prayer ministry.

Jesus did not want attention paid to his wonders because that could interfere with his work of bringing in the kingdom. It could short-circuit the preaching, teaching, calling and training he needed to do in order to build a disciplined cadre of followers. Our situation is similar. When signs and wonders are publicized, they can overshadow the good news and the work of the church. (They did exactly that in Wimber's church, which became obsessed for a time with miracles and prophecies.)

GREATER THINGS THAN JESUS

Walking in Jesus' steps means praying for those in need, asking God to provide for their deliverance. It means creating public opportunities: prayer meetings, prayer rooms, altar calls, prayer chains. It means letting people know that we love to pray for them and that we have faith God can help. When we let people know we are willing to ask for healing, they come.

We make ourselves available to do Jesus' work. We care for people by all means, in Jesus' name. That's because we are part of God's kingdom. Signs and wonders are natural where God's rule is known.

I want to say something that may sound blasphemous: if we have faith, we will do greater things than Jesus.

Jesus predicted that we would outdo him. "Anyone who has faith in me will do what I have been doing. He will do even greater things than these, because I am going to the Father. And I will do whatever you ask in my name" (John 14:12-13).

Jesus cannot be talking about miracles. Who could do more than he? His healings and miracles were spectacular. No one has ever come close.

In other ways, though, Jesus was limited. As a man of the first century he lived by the constraints of his time. He walked rather than riding in a car or plane. He spoke to crowds without sound amplification or TV. He might have invoked God's power to overcome these limitations, I suppose, but he did not.

Jesus' disciples did greater things when they spread the gospel beyond his small core of followers. They did greater things when they began to bless the nations beyond Israel, as the gospel crossed over into Greek society. As the gospel has spread throughout the world, the church has been able to do greater things many times over. From a group of just over a hundred, able to fit in one room, and all from one ethnic heritage, we have become a movement of two billion in almost every nation on earth.

And that is not all. Might modern medicine be included in the "greater things" that Jesus promised his disciples would do? Alexander Fleming, who discovered penicillin, has healed a hundred thousand times the number that Jesus healed. Any doctor today can heal more people than Jesus did. We have access to healing powers that Jesus did not.

Granted, modern medicine is thoroughly secularized. It typically offers no thanks to God. But does that mean God has taken himself out of it? I believe (and I think the Bible teaches) that he shows himself in every work of creation.

When penicillin was discovered, that brought gladness to God's heart. Everything good is part of God's kingdom, and we must take joy in it. If we see hungry people and know that we could feed them through agricultural development or heal them through vaccines or alleviate their poverty through economic development, how can we fail to extend our abilities? As children of the kingdom, it is in our nature to care for people in need, just as Jesus did. Such wonders are also signs of the kingdom.

PAUL BRAND AND MOTHER TERESA

Paul Brand was one of the loveliest men I have had the privilege to know. He served as a mentor to my friend Philip Yancey, and in some ways was the father Philip never had. I often heard Philip talk about Dr. Brand, as he always called him. Through Philip's eyes I saw Brand's gentleness, his humility and his wisdom—as well as his brilliance and creativity.

Brand was a world-famous hand surgeon. His wisdom was revered among world health authorities. Yet he made little money and lived modestly. He dedicated his life to healing victims of leprosy, most of them very poor. He made himself happy doing that work even in hot and difficult rural sites in India and Louisiana. He contributed greatly to the understanding of leprosy and to the practical therapy that enables leprosy victims to function effectively in the world.

Would Brand have showed God's grace more completely if he could have claimed some spectacular faith healings? Not according to me. I am sure he would have been overjoyed to see his prayers answered with wonderful healings, but he saw little of that. Yet surely Brand's work represents the flowering of Jesus' kingdom—blessings on the poor. He did Jesus' work in Jesus' way.

Consider a much more famous person, Mother Teresa. In 1948, she came across a half-dead woman lying in front of a Calcutta hospital. Knowing she could not save the woman, she stayed with her until she died. That experience led to a powerful sense of calling to serve those who were dying. At her own death, she had organized three thousand women to join her. They did not set out to heal people, but to love them to the end.

Would Mother Teresa have made a greater contribution to God's kingdom if she had been known for miraculous healing prayer? Actually, she was known for it. Part of the rigorous canonization process in the Roman Catholic Church involves the indication that wondrous healings are associated with the person proposed for sainthood.

Healing miracles are not her achievement, however. Mother Teresa became known to the world as someone who loved those who had outlived all usefulness and hope. She cared for the dying who had no one else to care for them. I know of no more beautiful sign of God's kingdom.

And now the world—especially the poor world—is in the grips of a terrible AIDS epidemic. It has already claimed more victims than any plague in history, overwhelming the resources of the communities it has struck. In some African villages only children and grandparents survive. The parents are all dead.

It happens that in many of the regions where AIDS is worst, strong churches exist. Right alongside this work of the devil, the power of the kingdom is available.

Furthermore, the world has become a global village, so that we in the West have access to those suffering. If the kingdom is really among us, will we not pour out help for the needy? Would not a great response to those afflicted with AIDS be a sign of God's power?

If the Holy Spirit were to provide healing from AIDS through the prayers of Jesus' followers, it would be a wonderful sign of the kingdom's presence. We ought to pray for people with AIDS, specifically asking God to heal them and thus show his glory. So far, however, it seems that the Spirit chooses to work more often through ordinary means—though I use the word *ordinary* with caution. When people show compassion toward those who are outside their family, isn't that a wonder? When medical researchers use their God-given talents to discover ingenious ways to heal, isn't that a powerful work?

WORKS OF POWER, DEEDS OF MERCY

I am trying to break down the difference, indeed the discrimination, between the natural blessing and the supernatural. The distinction is not to be found in Jesus.

To walk in Jesus' steps is to follow him in his everyday deeds of mercy. People ask; we respond. By doing so we show the kingdom's reality and power. None of us can do exactly what Jesus did. On the other hand, we really can do "greater things" than he could, just as he promised. Both impossible wonders and "doable" works of compassion demonstrate the coming of the kingdom, when they are applied with love and faith. "On earth as it is in heaven."

10

PRAYING

JESUS PRAYED. PRAYER WAS PART OF his public ministry, as when he prayed for little children (Matthew 19:13) or for a boy with convulsions (Mark 9:29). He prayed for his disciples—for Peter, that he would stand through testing (Luke 22:32), and for all the disciples as the crucifixion approached (John 17). Most often, though, the Gospels draw attention to Jesus praying in solitude. "Jesus often withdrew to lonely places and prayed" (Luke 5:16).

Think of a politician one week before an election, and you will be close to picturing Jesus' busy life. His entourage of followers never left. He had to juggle many agendas. Perhaps that's why the Gospels make special note of his going off alone, frequently at night. He balanced the crowded demands of daily living with times of solitary prayer.

Most Christians, I believe, have absorbed this lesson, at least in theory. We know we ought to set aside time to pray, even if we find it difficult to do so. But a further question arises: how did Jesus pray?

We pray, typically, about our worries—jobs and illnesses and examinations. We want to know whom to marry and how to make our lives happy. Surely we ought to pray about these things. It is our joy to talk openly with God about anything that troubles us.

If we want to pray like Jesus, though, we will pray with the consciousness he brought to the world, a consciousness of God's kingdom. Jesus' instructions in praying show us a way to raise our concerns to another level.

PRAYER LESSONS

When Jesus' followers asked him to teach them how to pray (Luke 11:1), they did not ask as beginners who needed basic instruction. The disciples were Jewish, and they had grown up in a community of prayer. They knew how to pray, having done it all their lives. Their request was more like asking Albert Einstein how to do math, or Leo Tolstoy how to write. Wouldn't you want Jesus to give you lessons in prayer?

Answering their request, Jesus gave a short model prayer. It is easily memorized, and many people use it as an outline, taking each phrase as a cue for expanded prayers on that subject. For example, after "Hallowed be your name," they offer praise and adoration. After "Your kingdom come," they name specific people and places where they want God to bring his power to bear. Each of the phrases in the Lord's Prayer can be folded out and expanded in this way.

Folded out, but not bent in an entirely different direction. The Lord's Prayer focuses on the kingdom of God. It is entirely a "family prayer" that offers not one word about individual concerns.

This may come as startling news. Christians have been praying this prayer for two thousand years, often—if my own experience is any guide—substituting individual needs for the kingdom needs. When we say, "Give us this day our daily bread," we unconsciously translate to, "Give me this day my daily bread." When we pray, "Forgive us our debts," we transform it to, "Forgive me my debts." We are such individualists that we instinctively turn Jesus' kingdom campaign into our personal religious journey.

If we want to pray the way Jesus taught us, we must recapture his original meaning. Jesus' prayer had to do with the urgent agenda of the kingdom he announced to Israel. It becomes our agenda when we join Jesus' band of followers. Personal, individual needs have to find place within the band's agenda.

Our Father in heaven. I used to think that this phrase was all about God. I heard it as a term of address similar to "Mr. President" or "Your Highness." By addressing God as a heavenly father, Jesus emphasized God's kindness and his close intimacy. He brought God near in a family relationship.

I realize now that "our Father in heaven" also identifies us, the people who pray. The first person plural possessive—"our"—is an odd little word in this context. To address a parent we usually just say "Father." "Our Father" is grammatically appropriate only when the family has gathered. Picture a family consultation, in which the children have come to talk to their father about family business.

In Jesus' day, it was Israel's privilege to pray, "Our Father." God had given the family its birth. He had taken a nondescript nomad and made his descendants into a nation with a unique, divine destiny. Israel could pray to "our Father" about this family destiny and the concerns that rose out of it.

Today the church takes up the same prayer. Adopted into the family of Israel, we have come into the family council to join Israel's conversation with our Father. If personal and individual concerns come up, they must be related to the whole family's situation.

Consider this: my three siblings and I have gathered for a serious conversation with our mother about her house, which we will jointly inherit. In the middle of the conversation I start asking my mother if she will lend me fifty thousand dollars to remodel my house. When one of my siblings asks me what that has to do with the rest of the family, I say it is strictly a private matter between my mom and me.

I would be obviously out of line. A family conversation is for family business.

When we begin with "Our Father in heaven," we assert that we are not addressing God with our own personal views, but we are speaking as part of the family. We acknowledge that our family perspective takes precedence and that our personal needs must fit within this. It amounts to a statement of loving humility: our humility before God our Father, our humility as part of a family that has concerns wider than ours as individuals.

Your name be holy. "Name" has to do with reputation, as in the phrase, "He has a good name." Praying this, we state our desire for God's reputation to be good. We want a tone of respect to come into people's voices when they speak of our Father. We revere God, and we want the whole world to share that respect.

Whether that happens depends largely on us, his family. A father's reputation depends on the lives of his children. If my siblings and I do well, our father's name will be well spoken of in our communities. If we live dreadful lives, you can be sure that our father's name will be treated with less respect.

With this prayer we commit ourselves to the kind of life that enhances our Father's reputation. "Live such good lives among the pagans that, though they accuse you of doing wrong, they may see your good deeds and glorify God on the day he visits us" (1 Peter 2:12).

When Christians are caught in immoral dealings, financial scams, sexual scandals or implacable disputes, they bring God's name into disrepute. On the other hand, when Christians care for the needy, respond humbly to an attack or create beautiful works of art, they make a name for themselves. Through their good work God's name gains a special status. We often rank our churches by number attending, number baptized, size of budget. I doubt such numbers cause the world around us to recognize our God as "holy." They suggest business as usual in a numbers-driven world. When a church practices sacrificial love, however, God's name is truly set apart.

Your kingdom come; your will be done on earth as it is in heaven. Jesus prayed this to dovetail with his announcement that the kingdom of God is at hand. Notice that the kingdom does not top off in heaven. It comes to earth. We pray that all the promises to Israel come true here in this world where we live.

That aligns closely with Jesus' longest recorded prayer, which he prayed for his disciples the night before his death (John 17). Jesus prayed for the long-term effectiveness of his campaign. He prayed for the faithfulness of his followers to go through temptations and to come out the other side unified and seeing his glory. Jesus had a vision for the kingdom come to earth through his followers. As he approached the cross, that was his concern and his prayer.

If my sister is desperately sick, I will surely pray for her healing. But if I follow in Jesus' steps, my prayers will place the illness in the context of God's kingdom and his goals. Healing can demonstrate God's power, his kingdom already at work on the earth. Healing can lead to praise, the prime activity of those who live in God's kingdom. I ask for healing not only for my sister's sake, but because her healing would advance God's kingdom.

Only once that we know of did Jesus pray for his own personal needs—the night before his death. He prayed for what he desperately wanted—escape from death—"if it is in your will."

I have heard people object to using that phrase in our prayers.

They say such a prayer may display mere fatalism, a lack of faith. "If it is your will" may become an escape clause, a polite and pious way to let God off the hook in case our prayers go unanswered. This objection is partly right, I think. If you throw in "if it be in your will" to insure against failure, you are not praying as Jesus did.

We can use the phrase in another way, however. It can represent a probing, meditating consciousness of something larger than personal happiness. We know we are not the center of the universe. Rather, the center of the universe is God. He is working to bring the entire cosmos to a good end. The way to that end goes through many dark passages; it involves suffering and pain as well as healing and joy. We do not see clearly how God is leading. Nevertheless we want to place our lives at the center of this great God-centered activity, over and above our own short-sighted interests. "Lord, let me find my place in your plan. Not my will, but yours be done. Your kingdom come, on earth as it is in heaven."

Give us today our daily bread. This request triggers memories of the Exodus, when the entire nation of Israel left slavery in Egypt for the Promised Land. Along the journey God gave them manna to eat, miraculously supplying what food they needed. It's easy to imagine the Israelites waking up in the desert and praying this prayer before they went out to gather the manna: "Give us today our daily bread."

We too are a people on a journey. In this prayer we ask for a repeat performance. "Supply your family with daily bread, just as you did during the Exodus. Provide us with all we need during our long journey into the promised kingdom."

The prayer has both a physical and a spiritual meaning. We need food to eat, real food. God knows our bodies' needs, and we depend on him to provide. Just as much, we need "the Word of God" because "man shall not live by bread alone." Praying this as a family, we ask

God to guide our church. We ask for strength and courage to enable us as a body to serve his kingdom well. We ask for good leadership. We ask for the resources to serve him. We ask not for what we want, but for what we need each day.

Forgive us our debts. In Jesus' day, this request had to do with Israel's national crisis. Even though Israel had come back physically from exile in Babylon, the nation was not restored to its glory. They had no king, and no prophets spoke the Word of God to them. Obviously, their sins still separated them from God' full blessing. They carried a debt, and it had not been forgiven.

Jesus' followers requested, therefore, that God forgive that debt. "Show us your love and your favor again, even though we have alienated you. As a people we have failed you again and again, but wipe clean our record and make us once more your favored people."

This is a church prayer. Individual sins contribute to our corporate debt, but the problem is not just individual. We are in this together. We need forgiveness together because we fail to do God's will together.

For example, we carry a history of racism and exclusion. Too often that debt keeps our church isolated from the people God wants us to care for. As a result, church becomes a social occasion for like-minded people rather than a gathering in which the power of God for his mission on earth transfuses our hearts. "Forgive us our debts so we can be restored to the mission you call us to."

As we forgive our debtors. Perhaps the most controversial phrase in Jesus' prayer, this suggests that Israel cannot be forgiven unless she gives up bitterness toward her neighbors. This was a hard word for Israel. Forgive the Romans, who look down on us and mistreat us? Forgive neighboring peoples who take pleasure in seeing our downfall?

Yes, we must forgive them. All debts must be forgiven—those we owe and those owed us. The kingdom of God is debt-free.

The so-called imprecatory psalms, in which Israel prays for God to kill her enemies, may remain in the prayer book but they can no longer be prayed. Jesus wants his disciples to turn the other cheek. He wants Israel to be known not for heroic resistance to foreign imperialists but for forgiveness. As Israel loves and embraces her enemies, God will forgive Israel and return to her.

This will be so for us just as for Israel. Whenever and wherever we are tempted to be bitter and angry toward our neighbors, we must forgive. Otherwise we will not get to experience God's forgiveness.

Keep us from temptation, but deliver us from evil. "Simon, Simon," Jesus said, "Satan has asked to sift you as wheat. But I have prayed for you, Simon, that your faith may not fail. And when you have turned back, strengthen your brothers" (Luke 22:31-32). The "you" that Satan will sift is plural in Greek—all the disciples. Simon's individual role is to live by faith through the sifting and, after repenting, to strengthen the other disciples. Evil attacks the whole family. Jesus prays that the individual disciple, having survived, will help the others. The whole band of disciples must be kept from temptation and delivered from evil.

When we pray, therefore, our focal point should not be merely our own personal deliverance from evil, but the church's. Our personal victories are meant for the common good. How can I strengthen the whole church?

For yours is the kingdom . . . This whole prayer is about God and his purposes. Our plans must fit into his. We offer ourselves as part of God's kingdom. We seek to become the kind of family God has in mind. The kingdom is his, not ours.

ROOM FOR THE INDIVIDUAL

It is not wrong to take Jesus' prayer as an outline and use it to ask God for our own personal needs. God loves not only the family but every member of the family. The family's needs come to ground at the individual level, and each individual need has a place in God's plan.

What we should not do is fracture the family prayer into a million individualized prayers without a larger sense of Jesus' mission. Jesus came to announce and to create a renewed people under God. He did not simply intend a new opportunity for individual personal growth or mystical spirituality. He had in mind the glory of a family under God.

The early Christians always prayed as a family seeking the kingdom. Look at Paul's prayers in this light. The prayers are intensely personal, but they focus on the welfare of the whole church. Paul prays for his friends as members of the church, with a view to their knowing "the hope to which he has called you, the riches of his glorious inheritance in the saints, and his incomparably great power for us who believe" (Ephesians 1:18-19). In short, he prays that they will experience the kingdom together.

That is what Jesus cared about, worked, suffered and prayed for. He taught us to pray in the same way—for the kingdom.

If I understand the Scriptures correctly, Jesus still prays for us in that light every single day (Romans 8:34; Hebrews 7:25). I imagine that he prays just as he prayed for Peter: that we will stand our sifting by Satan and learn to strengthen our brothers and sisters. Most probably Jesus continues the prayers for us recorded in John 17:20-24, that we will stand together and be united to him and his Father, seeing his glory. He prays for us as we carry on God's plans for an earthly kingdom.

I want to join that prayer, in the steps of Jesus, every single day.

11

WARNINGS

LIFE WAS HAPPY FOR JESUS' FOLLOWERS, at least in the early days. Jesus announced blessings and told stories of celebrations and homecomings. The great good day had come, he said. God's ancient promises were being fulfilled right now. He began to live out those promises by healing, forgiving and restoring people to the community of God's people. Jesus called followers to walk in his way of peace and to train others to do the same. Altogether Jesus' ministry was "good news."

We see this Jesus portrayed in a great deal of Sunday school art: Jesus as something like the Pied Piper, leading a parade of happy children.

Yet there is another side to Jesus. He issued warnings, sharp and dire. Like Jeremiah or Amos before him, like most of the prophets in Israel's history, Jesus warned sternly against groups of people as well as against certain attitudes. Some people took offense, believing that his warnings were pointed at them.

Jesus particularly criticized leaders of Israel, "the scribes and the Pharisees." He went after them aggressively, and they responded in kind. He might have avoided their enmity, dodging their questions and staying out of their way. With a little effort, Jesus could have stayed on good terms with everybody. (He never quarreled with the Roman authorities until the very end of his life.)

Instead, Jesus sometimes went out of his way to spark a dispute. For example, he called on a man with a withered hand to come forward in the synagogue, knowing that the Pharisees were watching disapprovingly to see if Jesus would heal on the Sabbath (Luke 6:6-11). On another occasion Jesus went into the holy temple and threw furniture around in a symbolic protest. In one of his longest speeches Jesus catalogued the Pharisees' shortcomings in devastating detail (Matthew 23). He made no attempt to soften his condemnation.

Obviously, Jesus considered these criticisms an important part of his work. Yet they make people uncomfortable. How could the Kindest Man Who Ever Lived behave so abrasively?

CRISIS AND OPPORTUNITY

Let me note that when I was a boy my mother and father issued stern warnings to me. Parents do that to their children. As the author of Hebrews noted, "What son is not disciplined by his father? If you are not disciplined . . . then you are illegitimate children and not true sons" (Hebrews 12:7-8). Parents do not study the failings of strangers on the street, but of the people they love.

So Jesus' warnings were never aimed at the pagan nations surrounding Israel, nor at harsh Roman occupiers. He warned his own people. His chief concern was that his community not shrug off his good news. He and his traveling band represented a choice and an opportunity that could not be put off. God was coming back to Israel now. Any individual, any group that failed to respond was in danger of being left behind in the darkness. The matter was highly urgent.

Thus Jesus singled out cities where he had preached. "Woe to you,

Korazin! Woe to you, Bethsaida! . . . And you, Capernaum, will you be lifted up to the skies? No, you will go down to the depths. If the miracles that were performed in you had been performed in Sodom, it would have remained to this day. But I tell you that it will be more bearable for Sodom on the day of judgment than for you" (Matthew 11:21-24).

Jesus told stories to underline the point. In the parable of the tenants (Matthew 21:33-46) a group of sharecroppers fails to welcome their landlord when he returns from a long absence. In fact, they rebel and kill his son because they want the land for themselves. They are suitably punished, and the land is given to someone else.

The parable of the wedding banquet, which follows (Matthew 22:1-14), tells of people refusing an invitation to a king's wedding, or else attending without bothering to change into suitable clothes. They too are harshly punished when they fail to respond in a timely and appropriate manner.

If your landlord is returning to his land, Jesus says, you must welcome him—or else. If your king invites you to his banquet, drop everything and go—and be sure you are properly dressed. We are living this parable, Jesus says. These events compel a response from every last person—not tomorrow, but today. Nobody can ignore the announcement and the invitation.

These warnings fit precisely with Jesus' good news. He announced that God, who owned Israel, was returning to his beloved land. He invited Israel to the wedding party in which God was claiming his bride. To refuse the invitation was to separate yourself from God and his good news. It was to place yourself outside God's plans.

Jesus warned all of Israel through these parables and others. There would be, simultaneously, a reckoning of accounts and a fabulous celebration. Everyone is invited and everyone must answer. Beware of being too busy to come at the summons of the king! Beware of being improperly dressed or of failing to do your work in preparation! The consequences will be disastrous.

I remember a friend in college who discovered to his horror that Jesus spoke often of judgment. He could not see how Jesus could be loving and yet so full of dire threats.

Of course, if nothing of consequence ever happens, nice people don't need to utter grim counsel. But important turning points demand dramatic warnings. History offers certain choices to us, and woe to those who choose wrongly! Nobody accuses Winston Churchill of unkindness because he warned of terrible consequences if England failed to prepare for Hitler.

Jesus lived in history. He did not float in a cloud of spirituality but walked on an earth filled with possibilities and dangers. He spoke of great good news, the fulfillment of all God's promises to Israel. But he saw that his people were poised to reject it and go the wrong way. He would do anything in his power for his beloved people not to miss the opportunity. So he uttered warnings—warnings of terrible consequences for those unready to welcome God's arrival.

WARNING IN HIS STEPS

Over the main entrance to many European cathedrals is a stone carving that attempts to communicate Jesus' warnings in picture form. It is a scene of the final judgment. On one side are those judged and damned to torment, carried off by hideous demons. On the other are the blessed, ascending to the realm of Jesus. The damned may be portrayed as priests, kings and even popes. Nobody is exempt from God's requirements, the carvings say. They remind parishioners every time they enter church that life is a choice between the most extreme outcomes. It is as though to say, with a giant exclamation point, *Pay attention!*

That same urgency has also been a staple of many sermons throughout history. Until comparatively recent times, preachers warned people to prepare to meet God. "Hellfire and damnation" were classic themes. Years ago, when I was researching a book on aging, I interviewed seniors who had strong, clear memories of such sermons. They had grown up with a God of wrath, some said. They associated church with fear.

Jonathan Edwards's famous sermon, "Sinners in the Hands of an Angry God," is exactly that kind of message. He spoke at the height of a remarkable revival, when hundreds of people were coming to faith in Christ. As historian George Marsden writes, "Being in the hands of God means for the moment you are being kept from burning in hell as you deserve. God in his amazing long-suffering is still giving you a chance; his hand is keeping you from falling."

The most famous passage of Edwards's sermon reads like this:

> The God that holds you over the pit of hell, much as one holds a spider, or some loathsome insect, over the fire, abhors you, and is dreadfully provoked; his wrath towards you burns like fire; he looks upon you as worthy of nothing else, but to be cast into the fire; he is of purer eyes than to bear to have you in his sight; you are ten thousands times so abominable in his eyes as the most hateful venomous serpent is in ours. You have offended him infinitely more than ever a stubborn rebel did his prince; and yet 'tis nothing but his hand that holds you from falling into the fire every moment: 'tis to be ascribed to nothing else, that you did not go to hell the last night . . . but that God's hand has held you up: there is no other reason to be given why

you haven't gone to hell since you have sat here in the house of
God, provoking his pure eyes by your sinful wicked manner of
attending his solemn worship: yea, there is nothing else that is
to be given as a reason why you don't this very moment drop
down into hell.

Oh sinner! Consider the fearful danger you are in.

Before the sermon finished the congregation was moaning and
crying out. "What shall I do to be saved?" "Oh, I am going to hell."
"Oh, what shall I do for Christ?" Shrieks and cries were heard so that
Edwards could not finish the sermon over the noise.

The sermon was widely printed in its day, and it is still widely
printed but for very different reasons. In the eighteenth century the
sermon was admired for pressing a spiritual crisis. Today it is read as
an example of hysterical and fanatical Puritan religion.

NO HINT OF WARNING

In times like our own, when people insist on living their lives without
interference from morality police, neither Jonathan Edwards nor
Jesus the prophet is an attractive figure. If we attempt to walk in
Jesus' steps by issuing warnings, we will encounter fierce resistance.

I cannot imagine a church putting the Last Judgment over its door
today. I cannot imagine a pastor preaching like Edwards. Nowadays
Christians frame their message in relentlessly positive ways. "God
loves you and has a wonderful plan for your life" offers no hint of
warning or crisis. It sounds like a special gift has been reserved in
your name at the front desk. You need not especially hurry. The gift
will remain for you, at your convenience.

Yet the urgency of Jesus' opportunity is just as great today as it was
in the first century or the eighteenth. The gospel is not a "timeless

truth," available at our convenience. God's kingdom is a dynamic movement, pressing toward a climax in history. Today is unique. We can never know whether and when we will get another chance to respond. Perhaps we will be differently preoccupied tomorrow, too distracted to grasp an opportunity. Or perhaps our opportunity will have passed. The urgency is not so much a threat as a pleading. This is the hour of decision. Not to decide is to decide.

I do not suggest that we return to preaching fire and brimstone, trying to frighten people into the kingdom of God. Our emphasis should be like Jesus': on the wedding banquet, the feast, the forgiving of debts. To follow in Jesus' steps means to tell about a kingdom full of joy and fulfillment. But let us capture the full urgency of his offer. How terrible to be left outside in the darkness. "This very night your life will be demanded from you. Then who will get what you have prepared for yourself?" (Luke 12:20).

THE ROLE OF LEADERSHIP

Jesus' urgency applies particularly to the community's leaders. Jesus came to save Israel, and it was for Israel's leaders that he reserved his most scalding warnings.

To save a nation, you cannot avoid confronting bad leadership. Take any national election. Two candidates, an incumbent and a challenger, vie to lead their nation. Do they need to "go negative"? It may be the farthest thing from their natures. The two could probably live peaceably as neighbors. They might even play golf occasionally, keeping their politics out of it.

When the leadership of the nation is at stake, however, hard comparisons and criticisms must come. The challenger must critique the way the incumbent has led. He will criticize his policies as well as his personal leadership. Believing that the nation needs a change of direction, he must say why its present leadership is wrong.

The incumbent is similarly bound to criticize the challenger. If his inexperience and his naive policy prescriptions would lead the nation on the wrong track, the incumbent must say why he believes so.

For a more religious example, consider Martin Luther King Jr. King was not a bitter or complaining man. Read his speeches and you will find them full of inspiring comments on the promise of American democracy. Even so, King sought to change the direction of the American South. That meant explicit criticism of the men who led Southern society. He offered a sharp prophetic critique of their leadership and so incurred their enmity.

Think of Jesus in that light, and you begin to understand why Jesus issued strong personal warnings. Jesus believed that Israel's leaders were leading the people astray. So he warned against those leaders, clearly and strongly.

Leaders Going the Wrong Direction

Jesus' dispute with the Pharisees was not with what they taught so much as how they lived. Just before launching into his diatribe against them, Jesus told his disciples to "obey them and do everything they tell you" (Matthew 23:3). Jesus endorsed keeping the Old Testament law down to the smallest detail, which is just what the Pharisees insisted on (Matthew 5:17-20).

Yet Jesus knew that God was doing something new. The Pharisees wouldn't see it. They had their eyes fixed on the rulebook and missed seeing that justice, mercy and faithfulness were being fulfilled in front of them (Matthew 23:23). They had the mindset of the servant who buried his talent (Matthew 25:14-30). Afraid to lose the treasure they had, they would not look up to see new, wonderful possibilities. They were busy preserving the past while Jesus introduced the future.

The Pharisees believed in preserving Israel from pagan corruption. They saw a nation surrounded by forces that could swallow them up. One of the most inspiring stories in Jewish lore told of a mother and her seven sons tortured to death for their refusal to eat pork (2 Maccabees 7). Such dietary heroism had become the highest possible patriotism. By following the law with great care, by keeping kosher and preserving the purity of the temple, the Pharisees hoped to keep Jewish identity intact. The Jews' distinctive diet kept them from dissolving into the sea of Greco-Roman culture, which pushed at them aggressively from all sides.

Jesus saw, however, that this strategy only increased the tension between Jew and Gentile, a tension that would lead to war and to Israel's destruction. He wanted a different set of distinctives to mark God's people: love, suffering, forgiveness and generosity. Jesus did not fear that a pagan culture would wash over God's people. Not if the kingdom of God had come! Rather, he expected that in the fullness of God's kingdom, pagan peoples would come to Israel, seeking to share in its blessings. Jesus had a joyous, hopeful expectation rather than a defensive posture before a hostile world.

Rather than building high barriers around Israel, Jesus would lead in the way of love, turning the other cheek toward the violent Romans, reaching out in generosity to Samaritans and strangers. The Pharisees and teachers of the law led in a different direction. As far as Jesus was concerned, they led Israel astray.

Jesus warned his disciples against the leaven of the Pharisees, which he identified as hypocrisy (Luke 12:1). Repeatedly he called the teachers of the law and the Pharisees hypocrites (Matthew 15:7; 22:18). Hypocrisy is not a theological error; it is a moral fault. It means not living by your own principles. In the diatribe recorded in Matthew 23, Jesus said the Pharisees were preoccupied with their own prestige and well-being, not with following God. Happy to burden others with finely tuned regulations, they found ways to avoid any burden themselves. They claimed to want Israel's best, but in reality they cared most about their own honor and prestige.

Jesus' condemnation was brutal. We can understand it only if we see that Jesus was not addressing a theological conference. God had sent him to save his people. They were headed toward war with Rome and the destruction of Israel. Urgently, Jesus had to wrest leadership from the hands of the Pharisees and the teachers of the law. The Pharisees lacked the true godliness that would guide Israel through the approaching days.

As a matter of fact, Jesus' predictions of disaster came true within a generation. Israel was devastated in a war that permanently dismembered the state and its temple. Jesus' band, however, came through the cataclysm. Gentiles began to turn to them for wisdom—the wisdom of the cross.

WARNING AGAINST FALSE LEADERS

Pharisees are no more. They belong to history, and we really have no one to fill their shoes today. So what do Jesus' warnings against their leadership teach us? Is there anything to imitate?

We may start by noting that Jesus' warnings were for family. He said not a word condemning the Greeks and the Romans. Tax collectors, sinners and even Roman authorities like Pilate he never branded with a warning. He knew Israel's greatest danger came from leaders whose hearts were insincere. Non-Jews were, of course, without adequate knowledge of the true God. Why critique them for that? That's why they needed a renewed Israel to be the light of the world.

The apostle Paul focused inside Jesus' movement when he wrote to the Corinthians. "I have written you in my letter not to associate with sexually immoral people—not at all meaning the people of this world who are immoral, or the greedy and swindlers, or idolaters. In that case you would have to leave this world. But now I am writing you that you must not associate with anyone who calls himself a brother but is sexually immoral or greedy. . . . What business is it of mine to judge those outside the church? Are you not to judge those inside? God will judge those outside" (1 Corinthians 5:9-13).

Some Christians are very ready to critique outsiders while cutting slack for their own. I run into this all the time as a journalist. According to some, I should avoid exposing the faults of my fellow evangelical Christians. They, after all, are the "good guys." Don't mention the unbearable temper, the mansion in the hills, the mass resignation of staff, the marital scandal. For bad guys, however—secular humanists, liberals, pro-choice politicians—do not temper the criticism at all.

Jesus' way was very different. He saved his warnings for the leaders of God's people. We should do the same.

Having said that, we should be very cautious before we critique our leaders. We do not have Jesus' vision, and we can easily go wrong. We have seen plenty of rancor and criticism in the history of the church, much of it contributing no good. Few things are as ugly as Christians quarreling.

Two qualities in Jesus' warnings will help us. One is that he never singled out individuals. Jesus criticized the Pharisees in sweeping terms and warned his disciples against them. Yet he named no names. Find me a church quarrel that never gets down to naming individuals, and I will show you a church quarrel that has a point.

I would not claim that naming names is wrong. Prophets did it. Paul did it. Jesus, however, did not, and I think we do well to consider his course.

By opposing the Pharisees on principle but not naming names, Jesus kept the door open for individuals. Jesus ate with Pharisees and talked with them individually. Nicodemus was a Pharisee, yet his curiosity led him to Jesus (John 3:1). Paul, too, was a Pharisee committed to destroying the church, yet he became a Pharisee dedicated to Jesus.

Second, Jesus focused on hypocrisy. His deepest complaint against the Pharisees was not doctrinal but moral, that their lives did not match up with their own principles.

Hypocrisy is a terrible charge to make. It goes, however, to the heart of leadership. Hypocrisy among the people of God is far more dangerous than any threat from outside.

So with God's people today. The greatest danger comes from those on the inside of the faith who are not fundamentally devoted to God. Some leaders hold good theological opinions but are fundamentally greedy. They love acclaim and power. They lack deep compassion for the poor. They mouth slogans but never do acts of service or sacrifice. We need not—should not—name them, but we ought to warn against their hypocrisy. Unless we do, we cannot face the crisis of our time.

GERMAN CHRISTIANS

During the 1930s, facing an economic crisis, the German government lost its sense of direction and was taken over by the Nazis. This new government would not tolerate any opposition. Communists, homosexuals, gypsies and Jews were harassed and imprisoned. A deeply racial ideology began to spread, along with an insistence that citizens unthinkingly follow their leaders. The new government sought to control even the churches, trying to place Nazi leaders in official church positions.

Germany was a deeply pious Christian nation. It had many vital, Bible-believing churches. Although many Germans greeted Nazism euphorically, other believers were shocked by its extremism—especially when Nazi leaders tried to take over the church.

Pastor Martin Niemoller, a former German naval officer, openly opposed the Nazi program. People flocked to his church to hear him. A conference was called in Barmen, where Swiss theologian Karl Barth wrote a famous declaration of the church's loyalty to Jesus over any other authority. Much of the German church leadership signed the document, and for a time it seemed that Christians might put up solid resistance to the Nazification of Germany.

Then the government put the screws on, imprisoning Niemoller and threatening to impound pastors' pensions. The vast majority of pastors decided they were better off keeping quiet. Some Lutheran pastors came from a Jewish heritage. When the government stripped them of their pastorates, the church kept quiet. With a few exceptions, such as Dietrich Bonhoeffer, they kept their noses clean while Hitler and his Nazis led the nation to utter disaster. As Niemoller would say after the war, "Don't ask Germans whether they knew what the Nazis were doing. Ask whether they wanted to know." Most devout German believers did not want to know.

Had pastors spoken up, they might have made a difference. We will never know because they did not speak up. If ever a people was led astray—and not merely by its Nazi leaders, but by its Christian leaders—Germany was it. Pastors knew what was right, and they had the moral authority to lead their people. But they were afraid. They held on to their one talent, and as a consequence they lost everything.

Had they stood up for right, the church would have suffered but emerged from the war with a Christian testimony. As it was, Christians emerged ashamed, no better than the rest.

Surely that is a warning to us. We need not fear the world outside. But hypocrisy inside?

To walk in Jesus' steps would have meant warning not just against the godlessness of Nazism, but also against pastors and other Christian leaders who professed faith in God but cared more for their security. In some respects it takes more courage to criticize your friends than your enemies

GREED AND HYPOCRISY

I will speak of one area that stands out to me: the commercialization of faith. In America today, religion can be quite profitable. Christian business—in media, in seminars, in music, in cards and religious gadgetry—is lucrative. This may be the first era since the medieval papacy when a person can get rich through the practice of Christian faith.

I do not mean to suggest that people do wrong to make a profit. Even if people grow rich practicing ministry, I am not sure they sin. They do wrong when greed rises above the righteousness of the kingdom of God. Some of them publish books or develop seminars that pander to the Christian market. They know what people want to hear, and they provide it. Some are frankly cynical about the calculations of what will sell. Woe to them! Woe to publishers who are most concerned to catch a publishing trend. Woe to writers whose sales figures are their greatest source of delight. Woe to speakers who command such high fees that they never experience the grit of ordinary church life. Woe to Christian businesses that measure success by the bottom line. Nothing does more damage to God's kingdom in America than this commercialism. Can anyone imagine Jesus living this way? Greedy religion does not walk in Jesus' steps, and it undercuts those believers who seek to do so.

Where are our warnings about living in luxury while people in the same town go hungry? Who warns forcibly that political power can never build the kingdom of God, no matter how righteous the politician? Who pronounces woe on Christian leaders fascinated by and greedy for influence? Do we warn against smug racial and ethnic separatism in our churches that insulates us from a world of hurt and anger?

Warnings are uncomfortable. They were uncomfortable when they came from Jesus. Warnings provoke anger. Hardly anybody enjoys the conflict they provoke. Jesus shows us, however, the urgency of the kingdom when he warns against hypocritical leadership and laissez-faire attitudes. If we want to follow his steps in transforming the world, we must warn urgently against those forces that can lead us astray. The alternative is to become a self-satisfied, self-congratulatory community—salt that has lost its savor.

12

GOING TO JERUSALEM

NOTHING FORCED JESUS TO GO TO Jerusalem, where danger faced him, where his disciples knew he might get killed. Why go? What did he hope to accomplish?

He had carried out the vast majority of his ministry in the small towns and villages of the north, and he might have stayed with that approach. Israel was an agricultural nation, and most of its citizens lived in villages within easy access of their farms and flocks. Jesus could have carried on doing good in such places, preaching the gospel and avoiding confrontation. He could have reached a very large audience without ever setting foot in Jerusalem.

Yet Jesus set out for that city, predicting very openly that the Roman occupation would kill him there. He went into some detail about the future he saw unfolding: he would be betrayed to the Jewish leaders; they would turn him over to the Gentiles, who would beat and abuse and finally kill him. He would rise again on the third day (Mark 8:31; 10:33-34).

Jesus' disciples were mystified by these predictions. Peter tried to correct him, only to be called "Satan" and told to get out of his way (Mark 8:33).

Jesus' approach to Jerusalem created great excitement in the crowds, who thought that the kingdom was about to appear (Luke 19:11). His disciples were astonished and troubled. Other followers were frightened, presumably at the prospect of violence (Mark 10:32).

Jerusalem was "the city of the Great King" (Matthew 5:35). All Jews knew it as the capital, where the king lived (even if the throne had been empty for many generations). Also in Jerusalem was the temple, Israel's beating heart.

Jerusalem was all that Paris is to the French, London is to the English, and Washington, D.C., is to the Americans. It was Rome to Catholics and the Ganges River to Hindus. It was simultaneously God's home on earth and the city that killed God's prophets. Since Jesus had come to announce and launch God's kingdom, he had to go to Jerusalem. Any revolutionary would do the same. Could Lenin avoid Moscow? Could Mao Tse-tung stay in the countryside and ignore Beijing forever?

In that respect Jesus' decision is easy to comprehend. Yet he foresaw that his offer to transform Israel would be flatly rejected, and he would be killed. Why did he go, even knowing he would be defeated?

POLITICAL THEATER

Jesus not only traveled to Jerusalem, he made his entrance a spectacle. By riding in on a donkey, he deliberately called to mind Zechariah's prophecy of the Messiah:

See, your king comes to you,

> righteous and having salvation,
> gentle and riding on a donkey,
> on a colt, the foal of a donkey. . . .
> He will proclaim peace to the nations.
> His rule will extend from sea to sea
> and from the River to the ends of the earth.
> (Zechariah 9:9-10)

As political theater, this is on the level with a presidential candidate riding into Washington, D.C., on a tank. It was deliberately provocative. Jesus was offering himself—no, asserting himself—as king, and not only as king but as emperor of the earth, like Augustus Caesar. From sea to sea! From the River to the ends of the earth! Let no one say that Jesus lacked guts.

True, the donkey is a gentle animal and a striking contrast to a Roman conqueror's stallion. Zechariah's picture of the great king riding on a donkey is almost humorously mild. Israel's great king would be quite different from what people expected!

But then, everybody knew already that Jesus was no warrior. He had no troops, no weapons. He trained his disciples to love their enemies and to turn their cheeks rather than to retaliate. Jesus on a donkey is no stretch. It fits who he is.

Jesus acting out the famous Zechariah portrait, however, had shock value. In an act loaded with symbolism for Scripture-loving Jews, Jesus said in loud and unmistakable language, "I am king!" and "I have come to rule the nations!" People got the message. They began shouting, "Hosanna to the Son of David!" and "Blessed is he who comes in the name of the Lord!" (Matthew 21:9).

He went into the temple and began throwing furniture around, overturning the moneychangers' tables. Sometimes this is called the cleansing of the temple, but that terminology leaves something to be desired. Presumably the moneychangers were back at work the next morning, if not the next hour. Some cleansing! Jesus' action is better understood as a protest. This temple, he says quoting Isaiah, is not what God intended. God meant it to be a "house of prayer for all nations" (Mark 11:17), drawing the Gentiles to join in worshiping the one true God of Israel. Instead the temple stood as a symbol of Israelite separation and defiance. It repelled Gentiles rather than drawing them in.

Jesus also quoted Jeremiah 7:11 (Mark 11:17), in which God calls the temple a "den of robbers" as he condemns it to total destruction. This is not the language of cleansing but of impending obliteration. In Jeremiah's time God let the "den of robbers" be flattened. He would again.

What Jesus did in the temple is like burning the flag and pouring blood on the Tomb of the Unknown Soldier. No other protest would be so likely to incense Israel's leaders. The temple was Israel's holiest site. Who was Jesus to walk in and start turning over tables? Who appointed him ruler?

That was Jesus' point, of course. He asserted his royal prerogatives: riding into Jerusalem in a royal procession, putting a stop to temple business gone wrong. He forced the city—leaders and peasants both—to decide about him and his agenda. He stood in their face.

Jerusalem might have accepted him. It looked for one giddy day as though the ordinary people would. They cheered him as he rode into town. However, Jesus had already seen beyond their superficial reactions. Long before he saw Jerusalem's walls he told his followers that he would die there. He knew the character of humanity. He knew that Jerusalem would not embrace him as Messiah but would instead betray a fellow Jew to the enemy, turning him over to the Romans to be crucified.

Jesus saw his death coming and went steadily toward it. The extra-ordinary drama of the Holy Week story is not in some cat-and-mouse game that Jesus played with the authorities. The drama lies in his calm, constant march into the arms of his killers.

WHY DID HE WANT TO DIE?

Jesus believed that he was Israel's king, anointed by God to save Israel from her enemies like the great warrior-king David. He also believed that the victory must be done through sacrificial love, not through violence. In this he was unlike David. (Recall that God would not allow David to build the temple because he was a "man of blood" [1 Chronicles 22:8]). Jesus taught his disciples to turn the other cheek to their enemies.

The philosophy of nonviolence, as propounded by Leo Tolstoy, Mahatma Gandhi, Martin Luther King Jr. and others, is sometimes criticized for its limited application. It is one thing to march against governments with a conscience, such as British India. To march into the arms of the Nazis or the North Koreans or Al Qaeda is something else again.

Whatever one makes of this criticism, it does not apply to Jesus. He marched into the arms of Rome. This empire could—and did—line the roads with the corpses of tortured men. Romans took pride in their brutality, and Jesus had no illusions that they would act any differently toward him. Jesus' approach to Jerusalem had little in common with Gandhi or Tolstoy because he had no idea that he could convince the authorities to surrender power and back down from confrontation. Jesus did not appeal to the consciences of callous men like Pilate or Herod. He did not appeal to the chief priest or the leaders of Israel either. Jesus made his appeal to God, the only one he believed could save Israel.

By going to Jerusalem, Jesus forced a choice on Israel. They might, on the one hand, take him as their king and follow him in approaching Rome with love rather than hate. The religious scholars and temple officials might join with Jesus' band of tax collectors and fishermen, declaring to the great Roman Empire that they represented the welcoming light of the world. They could join Jesus in blessing, not cursing, their enemies. They could follow the way of love and see where it would lead. Thus they, joining with Jesus, would make their appeal to God. Only he could save them, and save the world through them, if they trusted him that way.

On the other hand, Israel could reject Jesus and condemn him. All Israel's sins and Rome's sins—worldliness and pride, violence and hypocrisy—would be turned against Jesus. They could crush him and all he stood for. Jesus knew that this would be Israel's choice and Rome's choice. Evidently he thought he could take it on himself, absorbing all its evil. He trusted God that if he, Jesus, would drink Israel's cup of poison and death, God would somehow redeem him and Israel through him. He would "rise again."

Jesus believed the Messiah was Israel's true representative. By going lovingly, obediently to the cross, Jesus would be what Israel should be. By accepting humiliation and death at the hands of Israel and Rome, he would absorb their sinfulness in himself and set them free.

From this deadly crisis Jesus expected transformation and, indeed, resurrection. He expected that Israel's sins would be expunged and a renewed Israel would emerge. He, as Israel's true king, would be first to rise.

ATONEMENT

I will leave it at that, for it is not my purpose to explain Jesus' atonement for sin. That Jesus believed in it I have no doubt: otherwise his willing death makes no sense at all. But how did the atonement work? Passages like Isaiah 50—55 or Romans 5—8 are rich but strain our understanding. Oceans of ink have been spilled in expounding them, and I doubt I can improve on what has been said. The mystery can be endlessly explained and perhaps never fully comprehended. How Jesus' death forgave Israel's sin, and ours, is a subject for the ages.

My subject is narrower: what Jesus did, and how we might follow in his steps. I have tried to understand the atonement, but as I have studied Jesus' life I have become increasingly impressed that he himself did not try to explain it. He did it. He told his disciples what he would do, and then he let them watch. He set an example, not so that they could themselves become an atonement for sin—that was his job alone—but so that they could learn to live like him. The sights and sounds of that Holy Week burned into their memories. The atonement became the focal point for their lives ever after—not so much a theological theory as the memory of Jesus on the cross and how that led to their liberation. By watching Jesus that week, Jesus' disciples learned how to live.

I met a woman in Sri Lanka who reminded me of Jesus. I drove with my friend Ajith Fernando far from the densely crowded roads of Colombo, Sri Lanka's capital city. When night fell we were still passing along a beautiful tropical seascape. Darkness enveloped the sky, and we traversed long stretches of landscape without seeing a single speck of light. But suddenly a bright envelope of greenish illumination appeared. In an open-air structure, perhaps a hundred women leaned over sewing machines under fluorescent lights. It was a garment factory, and they were making clothes for Target or the Gap.

Near midnight we reached Lalani's town, finding her church with some difficulty in the dark. Lalani welcomed us vivaciously. An attractive, motherly woman, she laughed and talked animatedly while showing us a family photo album. It included pictures of her wedding, photos of her husband's body after a gunshot had taken off part of his face, and snapshots of the blood left on their bedroom floor. There were also photos of the damage done to the church by a cluster of bombs. Lalani gave a running commentary on these and other photos as cheerfully as she would narrate her summer vacation.

Next morning the church filled up with worshipers. It was a simple cement-block building with benches for several hundred under a tin roof. Lalani had dressed in a white sari, and she led worship with effortless enthusiasm. I thought she seemed not only capable and wise but also very happy—deeply, unconditionally happy.

Over lunch she told me her story through Ajith's translation. Her husband, Lionel Jayasinghe, had been a Buddhist monk. He converted to Christianity after a tract caught his interest. Eventually he attended Lanka Bible College and joined the Assemblies of God. "He had a deep desire to come back to the area where he met Christ, especially when he learned there weren't any Christians in the area." He married Lalani in 1986, and they had a son the following year. The family lived in a very simple hut with no plumbing.

A small house church began to rise, but so did opposition. Local Buddhist monks went from house to house warning against the Christians. Death threats came in the mail, ordering Lionel to leave the community. On Friday, March 25, 1988, he and Lalani came home from visiting church members. Their eleven-month-old son was sleeping in their bedroom, watched by Lalani's sister. Hearing his parents come in, the little boy got out of bed, walking on his own for the first time. "Look at my little scamp!" Lionel said.

Lionel was called to the front door. Lalani heard a gunshot, and

Lionel staggered back into the bedroom, covering his face with his hands. Right behind him was a man with a knife, who repeatedly stabbed him. Lalani tried to shelter her son. She heard another gunshot. The intruder disappeared.

A car rushed Lionel to the hospital. Lalani said, "As they were taking him away I prayed, 'Lord, they didn't know what they did, please forgive them.' I later found out that just as I prayed those words, he breathed his last.

"They brought his body home, and I held onto his feet. He had received an award from Lanka Bible College for distinguished students. I prayed, 'I'm not a distinguished person like him, but I'm not going to leave here.'"

The Roof Burning

Afraid of further violence, Lalani's landlord asked her to vacate. When she moved to another small house, people threw stones at it day after day, frightening her son. Letters came telling her she would be killed like her husband unless she left by a certain date. Protests were organized against the church; the roof was burned down.

Ajith had earlier told me about this roof burning. He described seeing Lalani at a meeting in Colombo. When asked how things were with her church, she replied sunnily, "Wonderful! Praise the Lord!" Later she gave a more detailed report, telling how local opposition had that week organized a protest march and then burned down the church's thatch roof. Stunned by this news, someone in the meeting asked how it was that she said everything was wonderful. "Obviously," she answered enthusiastically, "since the thatch is gone, God must intend to give us a metal roof!"

"God became very close to me during that time," Lalani told me now. "I would tell him everything. I said, 'If you want me to die, I'm ready, but I'd prefer not, because I have work to do here. But if I die, I want to write on the wall with my blood, 'Jesus is alive.'"

Once when she went to preach in Colombo, a procession was organized against the church in her absence. Protesters forced those worshiping inside to surrender their Bibles, then burned the Bibles in a bonfire. (Lalani showed me a picture of the ashes.) The next morning masked men came and warned craftsmen working on a new sanctuary to quit. Fearing more violence, the church stopped building.

Church members warned Lalani that her child was in danger, and she finally accepted their judgment. "It was extremely hard," she told me, tears coming to her eyes. She wiped them and laughed. "When I dropped off my son [in Colombo] I was very sad. I told Satan, 'Your end is going to be a terrible end!' and then I felt better.

"Actually, my son is doing very well now." She laughed merrily again. "I should give a gift to those who threatened him, because he was struggling in school before he left."

In April of 1999, on Good Friday night, someone planted three bombs on the church property. Two exploded, harming no one but doing substantial damage to the sanctuary construction. "We didn't pursue any suspicions with the police. They would only beat up the suspect, which would bring more resentment." By this time Christians throughout Sri Lanka knew of Lalani. Contributions came in, and the church was able to complete construction on the new building, including a metal roof. Opposition mysteriously died out.

Lalani now counts twelve hundred believers where once there were none. (Seven house churches have started in the area.) She told me with considerable pleasure that the Assemblies of God recently put her in charge of the whole southern region of Sri Lanka. Her vision had been for 150,000 people in and around her town. "Now I'm praying for revival in the whole area!"

THE PERSISTENT WIDOW

Wherever Christians walk in Jesus' steps, they move instinctively toward their Jerusalem. Pastors like Lalani and Lionel go to regions where resistance is strong. They go innocently and peacefully, but they go persistently. They go prepared to suffer. Their very presence destabilizes the environment, no matter how lovingly they make their approach.

Jesus went to Jerusalem to say forcefully in deed and word, "I am king. You must decide." Lalani and Lionel went to a difficult place to say the same thing about Jesus. "He is king. You must decide." Respectfully and patiently they witnessed to him in deed and word. They went prepared to suffer the consequences. Jesus' Holy Week had burned a pathway for them to follow.

Such is witness. It explains why, as Jesus said, "Surely no prophet can die outside Jerusalem!" (Luke 13:33). Witnesses are drawn toward the place of confrontation.

The persistent widow of Jesus' parable is a model of witness done in Jesus' way. Like Jesus, she brings no power, no threat. She only brings her persistent witness to the truth, insisting that the most careless man in the world do justice. She goes repeatedly to her Jerusalem—to a powerful man who could not care less for her, for God or for justice. She cannot coerce him to listen, but she will not go away. The unjust judge eventually gives in, but as Jesus tells the parable, credit belongs to God. "And will not God bring about justice for his chosen ones, who cry out to him day and night? Will he keep putting them off? I tell you, he will see that they get justice, and quickly" (Luke 18:7-8). Luke says Jesus told this parable to encourage persistent prayer. Such prayer is related to persistent witness. The widow witnessed to the judge, and she prayed to God, who brought her justice.

My mind goes back to the civil rights movement. When black

preachers led a march from Selma, Alabama, to the state capital, they knew that the governor was a hard man, disinterested in justice, without fear of God or love of African Americans. Yet they marched to Montgomery, appealing to him. They knelt to pray on the highway while mobs of state troopers, agents of the governor, swept over them and beat them. Immediately after the beating, the preachers mobilized to march again. Do we have, in all our history, a better parallel to Jesus' parable of the persistent widow? And note: God brought them justice. The unjust enemies in power gave in.

Jesus' way is a peculiar combination of strength and humility. He went to Jerusalem, boldly and persistently making himself impossible to ignore. Yet he did not wield power to force his way ahead. When assaulted he made no retribution. He was ready to die if need be, trusting God to vindicate him.

For believers in a country like Sri Lanka, where persecution is real and prevalent, one may easily locate Jerusalem, the city that kills the prophets. In relatively tolerant Western countries, Jerusalem may not be so obvious. Where do the powers of hypocrisy and hostility come together? In Hollywood? Academia? The golf club? Is the capital city our Jerusalem? Or is it the house next door?

Take academia. If you are willing to keep your thoughts to yourself, nobody will bother you. Christians in the university can experience warm fellowship, wonderful worship and satisfying Bible studies. Only when they begin to speak up—regarding abortion, for example, or Jesus' unique authority—do they find that the tolerance of the university has severe limits. At that point witness begins.

Persistence, humility and love must come into play, as they did for Jesus. To respond in anger and self-righteousness is "human," and it may be "effective," but it is not the path of Jesus.

An example of witness comes from the evangelical student movement InterVarsity Christian Fellowship. In 2002, Harvard, Rutgers and the University of North Carolina at Chapel Hill withdrew recognition for InterVarsity campus chapters. All three chapters had a clause in their constitutions specifying that only evangelical believers could be officers. The universities held that these clauses were discriminatory and thus contrary to the university's commitment to diversity. In the name of religious diversity, the universities were prepared to banish it.

A *Christianity Today* article by Andy Crouch tells how InterVarsity responded in varied ways, by negotiating at Harvard, by entering public debates at UNC and by filing a suit against Rutgers.

> "That was a difficult decision, because we have never been a litigious organization," [InterVarsity President Alec] Hill said. "But at each of the three times when the Apostle Paul calls on the civil powers in Acts, he uses his rights to ensure that the church is strengthened when he leaves. We were compelled to go this route not just for our sake, but for the sake of other ministries."

In suing, InterVarsity wanted not so much to win as to get Rutgers's attention. They appealed for justice. The dispute was settled out of court, with Rutgers accepting InterVarsity's right to retain its religious faith while operating freely on campus. On all three campuses, in fact, university officials ultimately came around. Crouch notes InterVarsity's "combination of conviction and openness," which appreciates the university's emphasis on diversity while struggling for their right to be part of it. According to attorney David French, "The InterVarsity folks don't apologize for their beliefs, but at the same time they present the spirit behind the belief."

What stands out is InterVarsity's lack of rancor toward university officials, their willingness to appeal to the university's sense of fairness and to take the extreme public heat of criticism without lashing out in bitterness. Crouch warns that more such disputes will likely come, particularly over evangelical groups' unwillingness to condone homosexual practice. It will be tempting for Christian groups to retreat into the shadows or to embrace a harsh us-versus-them mindset. That is not how Jesus taught us how to live. Loving enemies means more than getting along while never discussing religion. It takes its shape through active engagement and appeal—the activity of the persistent widow, the appeal of Jesus as he went to Jerusalem to offer himself as king.

Here is how the apostle Paul describes witness: "We are hard pressed on every side, but not crushed; perplexed, but not in despair; persecuted, but not abandoned; struck down, but not destroyed. We always carry around in our body the death of Jesus, so that the life of Jesus may also be revealed in our body. For we who are alive are always being given over to death for Jesus' sake, so that his life may be revealed in our mortal body" (2 Corinthians 4:8-11). That is what it means to walk in Jesus' steps to Jerusalem. He offered his life to the unjust city that killed the prophets. They killed him, but God gave him victory.

He went to Jerusalem from love, to prevent Israel's destruction. He came to save his people from their sins, which had led them through exile to the brink of annihilation. He offered himself as their king, knowing his leadership would be spurned. He predicted death at the hands of the very people he came to save. Yet there in that great city, in and through his cruel and irrational death, came the victory of God. Jesus rose again, and a renewed Israel came to life. We who follow his steps are the fruit of that victory.

As we shall see in the next chapter, Jesus anticipated the fruit of victory the night before he died. By remaking the Passover he laid the basis of a renewed Israel, the people of God. They would be so closely identified with Jesus' death that they could be called "the body of the Messiah." Even before he went to the cross, he was thinking of us as the outcome.

13

SYMBOLIC LANGUAGE

JESUS' FINAL WEEK IN JERUSALEM was pitched to climax everything he had done. The city was packed with visitors. He marched in to the crowd's hosannas.

Yet on the whole, Jesus made few bold moves. He did not try, for example, to lead those crowds in a march on Pilate, the Roman governor. Mostly he did what he had done all along. He taught about the kingdom, often in parables. He spent time with his disciples.

Two activities were unprecedented, however: his temple protest and the New Passover meal that he hosted the night before his death. Both seem to be carefully calibrated moves. Jesus went to Jerusalem's most sacred site and made protest. He took Israel's most holy day and invented a new way to celebrate it.

Reflecting on these events has made me appreciate an aspect of Jesus' character I never knew. Jesus was a symbol maker. He used art to burrow into minds and hearts.

Repeatedly, and increasingly toward the end of his time on earth, Jesus did symbolic acts. Riding into Jerusalem on a donkey was one. Turning over tables in the temple was another. Washing his disciples' feet was a third. The Last Supper was the greatest symbolic act of all. Few if any works of art match the disturbing intensity of what he did.

Buddha had his begging bowl, Gandhi had his spinning wheel and his march to the sea, Churchill appeared jauntily on the streets of London while bombs fell. None of these symbolic deeds match what Jesus did. Philosopher Dallas Willard caught my attention when he called Jesus the smartest man who ever lived. The emphasis on intelligence is misplaced, I think, but I see Willard's point. Jesus was not just a good man. He was a great man. His extraordinary abilities are highlighted by his inspired use of symbols.

Indeed, following Jesus' example, Christians have a long history of using art to speak the truth. Cathedrals, stained-glass windows, illuminated manuscripts, poetry, murals, drama, song—these and many other forms have been used to witness. Nothing, though, speaks so powerfully and enduringly as the New Passover.

A JOURNEY TO MEMORY

My wife, Popie, likes to imagine future archaeologists unearthing our civilization and puzzling over the meaning of our stuff. Among our most precious possessions they would find boxes of photographs. How would they interpret these? I think they would understand us as a people desperate for memory.

My great-grandparents had perhaps a dozen treasured photographs. My grandparents had an album or two. We have photographs in drifts, boxes and heaps. CDs and hard disks fill up with digital images. Few of the photos have artistic merit. Weddings, reunions, birthdays, graduations—these important landmarks we try to capture like water in the hand. Photographs enable us to recall the precious moments so easily forgotten in the rush of events. To lose our photos is a terrible and irredeemable loss, which is why people often say that in a fire they would grab the photo albums first.

Memories are at the heart of a nation too. As an American I feed on memories of Martin Luther King, Abraham Lincoln, George Washington, John F. Kennedy. It is no accident that in America December 7 is solemnly noted every year. The shock of Pearl Harbor and the nation's response to it define our national sense of character and purpose. I am sure 9/11 will be remembered in the same way.

Every nation has its formative memories. Kenyans remember Jomo Kenyatta and the Mau Mau freedom fighters. Japanese recall the horror of Hiroshima. The French remember *liberté, egalité, fraternité*.

First-century Israel celebrated Passover year after year in memory of Moses' leading Israel out of slavery in Egypt. Though those events had occurred well over a thousand years before, Israel kept the memory alive through the annual Passover ceremony. Now Jesus planted a new memory, closely connected to the old. The apostle Paul's account of the New Passover, the earliest record we have, notes Jesus' words that this meal should be celebrated "in remembrance of me" (1 Corinthians 11:24-25).

RECREATING A NATION

It was no accident that Jesus chose Passover for the climax of his work. He might have chosen Yom Kippur, the Day of Atonement, when the sins of Israel were paid for by animal sacrifice. If Jesus' principal object was to work out a forgiveness transaction with God the Father, an appeasement of God's wrath, Yom Kippur might have been the better day. Passover suggests something more than forgiveness. Passover marks the move from an old, slave existence to liberation. It is all about leaving an old land and entering a new one. It speaks of recreating a people, which is precisely what Jesus meant to do.

Jesus told his disciples that he had eagerly anticipated celebrating

Passover with them (Luke 22:15). Presumably he had thought long and hard on how he wanted to celebrate. In the final night of his life, Jesus took the time-honored formulas of this holy day and bent them into a new celebration.

In the traditional ceremony, Israelites ate unleavened bread for seven days. On the final great day a lamb was killed and its blood splashed on the doorposts of the home. It was a family meal at which the events in Egypt were told aloud: how the angel of the Lord killed the firstborn son of every family that lacked blood on its doorposts, and how Israel was at last set free from slavery.

As Jesus took up the unleavened bread for his celebration with his disciples, he reshaped the old Seder meal around the event of his death. He said the bread was his body, broken. The wine was his blood, he said, poured out for the forgiveness of sins. In his New Passover celebration, Jesus offered a new memory for a renewed Israel, leaving slavery not through the death of the enemy's firstborn but through the death of God's firstborn, the Messiah. He placed atonement at the center of memory for a renewed nation.

Some scholars have contended that Jesus never intended to set himself up as something special. They say he only wanted to leave his wisdom behind, not to be worshiped as Savior and Lord. If you doubt that Jesus aimed to focus attention on himself, ask yourself this: why would he reshape the Passover celebration around "my body" and "my blood"? When we eat this New Passover meal, we remember him. Quite specifically, we remember his death. And more, we celebrate it. Through it we were set free from slavery to begin our journey to the Promised Land.

Sometimes Christians divide themselves between churches that are "sacramental," placing a high importance on ritual, and those that are "evangelical," stressing the mission-centered preaching of the gospel. At the Lord's Supper this distinction disappears. The Lord's Supper is certainly sacramental, a profound encounter with God and with God's people. We do not merely talk about communion with God; we experience it. We eat a meal together, a meal at which Jesus is the host.

At the same time this communion is an evangelical proclamation: Jesus died to set you free. Every time we take Communion, we participate in announcing the gospel through great art. We fix the memory of Jesus eating with his disciples as he went to his death and tying that death to Israel's liberation. As Paul wrote to the Corinthians, "Whenever you eat this bread and drink this cup, you *proclaim* the Lord's death until he comes" (1 Corinthians 11:26, emphasis added).

SUBSTITUTIONS

Napoleon was crowned emperor on a bitterly cold December day in 1804. It is said he planned the five-hour ceremony as painstakingly as one of his wars. Elaborate processions, fabulous costumes, wonderful decorations captured the attention of all Paris. Notre Dame cathedral, damaged and nearly torn down during the revolution, was commandeered to lend religious support to the event. The pope and his entourage were dragged all the way from Rome in order to attend and bless. Napoleon commissioned the great artist Jacques Louis David for a monumental painting. (You can see it at the Louvre today.) A medal was struck, showing Napoleon in a Caesar-like pose.

All this over-the-top ceremony was eclipsed, however, by one small innovation. Napoleon crowned himself. Rather than allow the pope or dukes and princes to put the crown on his head and endorse his authority, Napoleon simply lifted the pure-gold laurel wreath and did it himself. The symbolism said louder than words that Napoleon was one of a kind. Nobody granted his authority, only he himself. He bent a traditional ceremony to proclaim that he was beyond all tradition.

In his New Passover meal, Jesus also bent a traditional ceremony to new purposes. By using the traditional Passover meal, Jesus emphasized continuity with everything God had been doing in Israel. Yet startlingly new meanings arose from the old.

Liberation. The original Passover marked the drama of Moses calling Pharaoh to "let my people go." Israel left slavery in Egypt, setting off on a journey to the Promised Land. By launching a New Passover in Jerusalem, Jesus suggested that Jerusalem, too, might be a land of slavery from where a liberation journey must begin.

Promised Land, new kingdom. In Egypt the Israelites dreamed of entering a land God had promised them—a place where they could own property and make a settled existence. In recreating the Passover meal, Jesus redirected attention from Palestine toward the kingdom of heaven. The Promised Land could be anywhere that God ruled.

Necessary blood. The Passover began with blood, as the lamb provided a substitute for the firstborn sons who would die. The lamb's blood on the doorpost indicated that the sacrifice had been made. In calling the wine "my blood" and the bread "my body broken," Jesus put his own death as the new substitution.

Family meal. Unlike most Old Testament festivals, Passover took place at home rather than the temple. It was a family meal. By gathering his disciples for the New Passover, Jesus established a new family based on his calling rather than on blood ties. When Christians gather for New Passover, they proclaim themselves members of that family based on the name of Jesus.

In memory. Israel placed high priority on remembering God's great deeds. Passover set the liberation from Egypt as the centerpiece of Israelite history. By offering the New Passover as a celebration to be done repeatedly "in remembrance of me," Jesus placed himself and his death at the center of history. Since it is a Passover meal, we maintain our Jewish memory. We share with Moses, Joshua, David, Solomon, Isaiah and Jonah, all of whom ate this meal. Yet the meal takes a new meaning, recentered on the memory of Jesus' death as our sacrifice for sin.

In anticipation. New Passover not only helps us remember, it points into the future. The meal anticipates the messianic banquet, when all of God's people will eat together from one table. Jesus spoke of this great, final celebrative banquet in his parables, and he referred to it at the Last Supper (Luke 22:16). God's people are one people. There is no Jew and Christian at God's table. All those who accept his invitation will sit down for the feast together. Jesus affirmed the Jewish anticipation of a great celebration, and at the same time gave out party invitations to the whole world.

POSTMODERNISM

Although I grew up in a church that celebrated the Lord's Supper, I had a hard time conceiving of it as central to my faith. Understanding that Jesus had introduced it and told his followers to practice it, I still did not "get" it. I remember pondering why drinking thimbles of grape juice and eating tiny squares of bread was better than writing on a blackboard, "Think about Jesus" and taking ten minutes for silent meditation.

Perhaps that's because I grew up in an era of reductionistic science and rationalistic optimism. The search for truth was thought to be more accessible to nuclear physicists than to priests or artists. In most Protestant churches, the Lord's Supper became a quaint ritual. The sermon, an exercise in logical thought, dominated our attention.

Now the times have changed. Music, drama and art have matched sermons in significance. In a postmodern era people look to these for the most profound truths about themselves. They are not satisfied with cold propositions; they want those propositions fleshed out in story and song. Actually, this is not new but something ancient that has returned. From the time of the cave paintings, people have instinctively felt that poetry and art spoke to their true identity.

Jesus knew that and provided for it. His New Passover meal has become the most persistent and universal of all memory rituals. It has spread from that house in Jerusalem to the whole world. Jesus was a great symbol maker. He rewrote the Seder meal so his disciples might combine the new and the old, might encompass in one event their history with God from Moses on, the decisive culmination of that history in Jesus' death and resurrection, and their anticipation of the great final banquet.

The New Passover meal is not performed in a museum. It is celebrated by a community. On the night before his death Jesus anticipated the community that would form after his death. The New Passover would be the meal they gathered around to affirm their real identity in Jesus.

If Jesus made symbols, so should we. Protestants have historically looked askance at art because they saw it abused in the Middle Ages. But Jesus' example as a symbol maker suggests that art and ritual can and should be used to speak in ways that words cannot.

Whether we are artists or not, we follow in Jesus' steps whenever we participate in the Lord's Supper. He ate this meal, and so do we.

These are our family reunions. These are the memories that bind us together. These anticipate the great meal we long for. The New Passover takes away the possibility of going it alone, of make-your-own religion, of finding God in the forest instead of in church. The New Passover tells us that just as Jesus lived within a community of faith, following traditions (though certainly not slavishly) and putting up with the diverse, up-and-down reality of ordinary people (remember who those disciples were), so must we. This is Jesus' way. We are the people he died to save. The New Passover forms us as a people living in his kingdom. We represent his victory, his achievement.

FOOT WASHING

I once belonged to a church that believed the Lord's Supper should recreate Jesus' entire last evening with his disciples. Every few months our congregation came together to eat a fellowship meal, take Communion and wash each other's feet.

I had never practiced foot washing before I joined that church, and I confess it had no particular appeal until I experienced it. I particularly remember how strangely intimate the act seemed—so intimate, in fact, that for the sake of propriety men and women went to separate rooms to do it. I would have thought that silly until I participated in the deed. Washing someone's feet brings you very close together. You kneel before him, carefully removing his shoes and socks. You grasp his feet in your hands, massaging hidden calluses and soft skin with water and soap and towel. It is too close to be casual about. It brings a sense of almost shocking familiarity.

So it must have seemed to the disciples when Jesus took a towel and basin and silently began to wash their feet (John 13:2-17). The atmosphere was already charged. They had marched into Jerusalem knowing quite well that they put themselves in danger. Now Jesus, their Lord and teacher, was acting a slave's part. It seemed all wrong. He put his hands on their feet in disquieting intimacy. (When, if ever, did a dignified rabbi touch his disciples?) Further, he told the disciples that they must follow his example with each other.

His point was not democracy, that everybody should do his fair share of the dirty work. His point was slavery. In the kingdom of God you must become the slave of others, giving up status and privilege of every kind and placing others' welfare above your own. Slaves don't do their share of the dirty work. They do all of it—whatever needs doing.

Through foot washing Jesus clarified what kind of community he intended to form. He did not require his followers to become martyrs, flaming out in glorious self-sacrifice. He wanted slaves. Slavery offers no hint of glory, only service. Jesus used the New Passover as the basis for a new community formed around his death. Through foot washing, he showed unforgettably that this community lives by service.

QUARRELS OVER LEADERSHIP

Even before that last night, Jesus had talked to his followers about becoming slaves for others. Usually the context was an argument. The disciples had joined Jesus' movement hoping to reap rewards. They quarreled over future roles in the government. Two of them had a mother who went to Jesus with a special request—that her sons should be his vice regents. The other disciples were indignant when they heard about this power move.

Jesus called a meeting and told the disciples that they were acting like Gentiles (Matthew 20:25). On first thought, this seems unfair to Gentiles. He might with all fairness have said they were acting like Jews. Nothing in Israelite history suggested that Jews were exempt from power games. Jesus' point, though, was that power games are fundamentally alien to the kingdom of God. Jews might (and did) participate in such quarrels, but then they were not acting in a truly Jewish way.

What true Jew could Jesus cite as a positive example? What leader had served as a slave to others? Not Moses, humble as he was. Not Elijah. Not Samuel. Not David. Only Jesus himself. "The Son of Man did not come to be served, but to serve, and to give his life as a ransom for many" (Matthew 20:28). Jesus was the true Jew. This way, Jesus said, leads to greatness.

Jesus nailed home this message in his final night, picking up a towel and basin. It was an unforgettable symbolic act. This was the last night he would spend with them before his death. They would never lose this image of Jesus, so long as they lived. He considered it absolutely key to carrying on the kingdom.

Addressing the Weak

Significantly, Jesus addressed this message to men in leadership. He spoke to "whoever wants to become great among you" and "whoever wants to be first" (Matthew 20:26-27). The message of slavery spoke to those quarreling for precedence.

It would be trickier to address those lacking ambition and self-confidence, or those who must serve others because of their inferior social position. Jesus did not speak this message to lepers, women or slaves. They might hear the message of slavery as an endorsement of the social system. When we tell downtrodden people that they must be slaves, we risk serious misunderstanding.

Jesus certainly did not endorse slavery or any other social hierarchy. In his kingdom, all such systems are transformed. The slavery Jesus wants is voluntary. It has nothing to do with accepting your lot as an inferior. It means serving others, putting their needs ahead of your own. It is the way to greatness.

OTHER SYMBOLS OF SERVITUDE

A pastor I know recently went to Mexico. His son had asked him to go along with the youth group, which took its spring break building houses for the poor. The pastor in question heads a large church. His life is extraordinarily busy. The Mexico trip was sandwiched between four Easter services and a national board meeting he had to chair. Beside all that, the pastor hates camping. Sleeping on the ground and skipping showers was his idea of a nightmare, not an adventure.

He did not go to Mexico because he was needed. He knew that the regular youth staff would be more effective than he at communicating with the teenagers who went. He did not particularly expect to have great interactions with his son while in Mexico, nor did he believe that his ministry should include carpentry. He went because his son asked him to go. He went as a slave to his son.

That is a form of symbolic service. We do such service not because it is the best use of resources. Most probably it is not. Nor do we suggest that everyone, all the time, should do what we do. We do something unusual, even shocking, to make the point of service. Symbolic service communicates that we follow in the steps of Jesus.

Thus Jimmy Carter on his inaugural day got out of the presidential limousine and walked to the White House like a common citizen. It made no sense as transportation. It was symbolism, making a powerful statement about the presidency.

Thus my friend Gary, a college professor, greeted the freshmen every year as they moved into their dorms and helped them carry their luggage to their rooms. Of course eighteen-year-olds can carry their own luggage, but Gary did it to symbolize his eagerness to serve.

Some friends of mine took an American student mission team to Vietnam, where they engaged in a cultural exchange program with university students. They led discussions on many aspects of American society—subjects like national holidays, the American political system and American views on race and ethnicity. Though the Americans were all committed Christians, they never talked about their faith. The Vietnamese authorities had told them the subject was off limits. The Americans had gone to Vietnam through an organization that hoped to build long-term relationships, and so they felt obliged to obey the edict. Any fudging might spoil future chances for ministry.

Still, they looked for a way to share their most meaningful commitments. For a final celebration of their weeks together, they decided after much prayer and thought that they would speak in symbolic language, as Jesus had. They told the Vietnamese that they would like to share a tradition—one not familiar to all Americans but very important to them. They proceeded to wash the Vietnamese's feet.

Some of the Vietnamese flinched. They did not immediately understand what the Americans were doing. Some giggled uncomfortably. Eventually, though, the experience turned silent, solemn and quite emotional.

The Americans did not try to explain what they did or why. They counted on the deed to speak for itself. They hoped that someday those Vietnamese students would learn about Jesus' foot washing and connect it to their experience that day. Whether that happened or not, the American students hoped that by washing others' feet they conveyed their desire to serve, even at the cost of their own dignity. They hoped that the deed showed them as people who came in humility, not superiority.

SYMBOL AND REALITY

Ajith Fernando, who leads Youth for Christ in Sri Lanka, conceives

of his life as a slave to Christ, and furthermore as a slave to his fellow
human beings. That way of thinking is engrained into his life at all
levels, whether he is speaking at large international conferences or
writing Bible commentaries. I see it most dramatically when he waits
in line.

Sri Lanka is a very poor country, and it is bedeviled by ethnic and
class differences. It often happens that people fall afoul of government bureaucracy—whether with police, tax authorities, schools or
hospitals. These bureaucracies throw up barriers that an educated
Sinhala-speaking man like Ajith can sometimes surmount but that
people from other backgrounds may find utterly impenetrable. So
Ajith often is called from his highly demanding schedule to go stand
in line with someone who lacks his advantages. They wait to see a police inspector who can release a man arbitrarily jailed. They wait to
talk to a school principal about a child who cannot afford the fees.
They wait to see a tax authority or a medical doctor. The wait can last
for hours. Sometimes, after waiting for hours, they are told to come
back the next day.

Ajith is not averse to getting someone else to go in his stead. But
at times no one else can help as well as he can. So he goes and waits
long hours in line. He has to put off urgent work—meetings and de-
cisions and writings that demand his attention. Yet in his way of
thinking, nothing he does in leadership matters more than waiting in
line. Partly that is because he does something useful that no one else
can do as well. Partly it is because he is making a symbolic statement
to all his Youth for Christ staff, and indeed to all the Christian leaders
of Sri Lanka.

That is slavery. It is sacrificing your life for someone else's. It is also
leadership in Jesus' steps, using your life as a symbol of service. According to Jesus, you find your life this way and become great.

This mindset propelled Jesus to his death. He thought it so important that he taught it on his precious last night with his disciples. It should be just as important to us, if we want to follow Jesus' steps. It should mark the community that Jesus anticipated would arise to remember his death.

14

GETHSEMANE

WITNESSING TO THE TRUTH OFTEN leads to terrible suffering. It has done so through the ages, and it will again. We never go looking for it, but we would be fools not to prepare for it.

Gethsemane and Calvary show us how to live as people in the shadow of suffering and death. Confronting evil is not a political science technique. It is terribly and completely personal. Nothing in Jesus' life made a greater impression on his first followers than his behavior at his trial and execution. Peter cites Jesus' trial as a pattern for our response to suffering.

> Christ suffered for you, leaving you an example, that you should follow in his steps.
>
> "He committed no sin,
>   and no deceit was found in his mouth."
>
> When they hurled their insults at him, he did not retaliate; when he suffered, he made no threats. Instead, he entrusted himself to him who judges justly. (1 Peter 2:21-23)

We have seen Jesus as master of Holy Week: a king prompting a confrontation in the capital city, a symbol maker reshaping the memory of his nation. After the Last Supper with his disciples, however, he was no master, but a victim; not so much a king as an ordinary human being pleading to God for escape. He had chosen his destiny in absolute freedom, but now the death machine had lurched into inexorable motion.

Deep distress touched Jesus in Gethsemane. "My soul is overwhelmed with sorrow to the point of death" (Matthew 26:38). "And being in anguish, he prayed more earnestly, and his sweat was like drops of blood falling to the ground" (Luke 22:44).

Writing about this sorrow to his friend Owen Barfield, C. S. Lewis commented on why Jesus seemed so much more troubled than many brave men facing death.

> Ordinary men have not been so much in love with life as is usually supposed: small as their share of it is, they have found it too much to bear without reducing a large portion of it as nearly to non-life as they can: we love drugs, sleep, irresponsibility, amusement, are more than half in love with easeful death—if only we could be sure it wouldn't hurt! Only He who really lived a human life (and I presume that only one did) can fully taste the horror of death.

Jesus' horror went deeper and wider than personal loss. He was the hope of Israel. If he died, Israel died with him. And Jesus loved Israel. God had poured his life into these people, and they were about to turn on his messenger—his own Son—and betray him to the Romans. As they killed Jesus, they were killing themselves.

I doubt any of us can ever feel such absolute sorrow. We feel profound grief over our individual woes—the death of someone we love, for example. A national tragedy like 9/11 or an international disaster like the Indonesian earthquake and tsunami of 2004 can overwhelm us with astonished heartache. We see it, nonetheless, through narrow blinders of our own perspective. Our imagination is not large enough to encompass the whole world. Jesus' vision was so much wider and more penetrating that he saw Life itself carried to the point of death.

GETHSEMANE PRAYERS

Filled with this sorrow, Jesus did as he often did: he went off alone to pray. The Gospel accounts show him leaving his friends to pray and returning to them, leaving a second time and returning, then leaving a third time. It was as though he could not stop praying, and he could not stop turning to his friends.

His prayers were quite simple. He asked his Father, "May this cup be taken from me" (Matthew 26:39).

In the great prophets Isaiah, Jeremiah and Ezekiel, "this cup" is full of God's wrath. Ezekiel says that adulterous Judah must drink it.

> For this is what the Sovereign LORD says: I am about to hand you over to those you hate, to those you turned away from in disgust. They will deal with you in hatred and take away everything you have worked for. . . .
>
> This is what the Sovereign LORD says:
>
> > You will drink your sister's cup,
> >   a cup large and deep;
> > it will bring scorn and derision,
> >   for it holds so much. (Ezekiel 23:28-32).

Jesus must drink this cup for Israel. He will drain the large, deep cup all by himself. The most awful thing imaginable is about to happen to Israel, and Jesus will bear it alone. Israel is about to kill her best and only hope. Israel is about to kill her Messiah. They do not know what they do. Only Jesus knows.

Is there another way? That is what Jesus asks. He pleads with God to let the cup pass from him, while yet affirming, "Not as I will, but as you will."

Thank God we ordinary humans never experience such death and sorrow. Yet when we encounter bottomless sorrow, when all hope is shrouded in darkness, we should pursue prayer as Jesus did, "with his face to the ground" (Matthew 26:39). Those who walk in Jesus' steps must seek solitude to pray.

I wonder, in fact, whether we learn to pray in any other circumstance. For myself, so long as life goes well my prayers float on the surface, distracted, fragmentary, forgetful. Only facing desperation do I pray with sorrowful groans too deep for words. Sorrow presses me to the ground to pray like Jesus.

SEEKING SUPPORT

While Jesus prayed alone, he also sought support from his closest comrades. He took his disciples with him to Gethsemane, asking them to wait for him. He took Peter, James and John farther along, sharing his sorrow. When he returned from prayer to find his friends sleeping, he was terribly distressed. "Could you men not keep watch with me for one hour?" (Matthew 26:40). He knew they could not share the cup with him, but he wanted their physical presence, their prayer and their watchfulness.

His disciples were too weak for the situation, and Jesus knew it. He had warned Peter in advance that he would deny him. Still, Jesus urgently sought their company. Great as he was, frail as they were, he needed them. He relied on their fellowship and never

scorned them for their weakness. He sought their company as far
as they could go with him on his pathway.

So we must do, too, when we walk in Jesus' steps. We can turn
only to people as weak as those disciples, or weaker. If we look for
support in church, our fellow believers will fail us. When we seek
company in our suffering, they will go to sleep. And yet we must be
like Jesus, seeking the fellowship of those who will walk with us as
far as they are able.

A good friend of mine lost his eight-year-old daughter a few
months ago. We meet regularly to talk, and day by day, week by
week, I have seen his grief. He has suffered a wound he can never forget, but months (or even weeks) after the death, others have moved
on. He feels that his emotions are embarrassing and unwelcome to
others. "Isn't it time that you get over it?" people seem to ask. But he
cannot move on.

Despite the pain this causes him, my friend repeatedly makes himself vulnerable to others. He knows that he cannot heal properly
without their company. He needs their support and prayers, so he
speaks openly of his daughter and the pain he feels. He asks for
prayer. He does not isolate himself in his pain but rather seeks Christian company. In doing so, he follows Jesus' steps.

Today we see the rise of a new phenomenon, the "unchurched believer." According to Barna Research, ten million self-proclaimed
born-again Christians in America have not been to church in the last
six months. They consider themselves real believers, yet they have no
real connection to church.

A common complaint from such believers is that when they were
in trouble, the church failed them. Perhaps so. The church is not
made up of better people than the Twelve. But knowing how those
twelve would fail him, Jesus still leaned on them for strength and

comfort as he faced his hardest hour. If we want to be like him, we will do the same. Like Jesus, we will go back to them twice, even three times, wake them from their sleep and ask, "Will you watch with me?"

BETRAYAL

Have you ever felt betrayed by a friend? Have you learned, for example, that someone you trusted to support you has been undercutting you instead? That someone you cared for has gone out of her way to hurt you?

I know nothing more galling, more likely to produce white-hot anger. The reversal of feeling, from trust through shock to bitterness, burns your vitals.

Jesus was deep in prayer when Judas, one of the Twelve, betrayed him. "Greetings, Rabbi!" he said, kissing him (Matthew 26:49).

If Judas had lost faith in Jesus, he could simply have left. Instead he turned Jesus in for money. Yet Jesus responded without an embittered word. "Friend, do what you came for," he told Judas (Matthew 26:50). And, gently, "Judas, are you betraying the Son of Man with a kiss?" (Luke 22:48).

Those who walk in Jesus' steps will accept betrayal, gossip and all kinds of mistreatment by their friends. They will not retaliate. They will, as Jesus taught his disciples, turn their cheek to receive another blow.

ARREST AND ISOLATION

A close friend of mine was arrested last year. He made an egregious misjudgment in handling a financial matter. An elderly friend had turned to him for help with financial management, and he had not kept good records. Then his elderly friend's son began to attack and accuse. My friend's actions had been honorable in intent, but held to the light by an angry son they looked questionable. My friend was charged with elder abuse and arrested at his home. The police handcuffed him in front of his children, put him in the back of a squad car and left him there for forty-five minutes in plain view of the neighbors. After they had thoroughly humiliated him, they took him downtown and booked him. He spent twenty-four hours in a holding cell before being bailed out.

Ultimately my friend was vindicated. The arrest was expunged from his record. However, I doubt whether anything can expunge from his mind the helplessness and shame of that arrest.

Jesus was arrested under cover of darkness by men who had listened to him teach all week in broad daylight. They brought swords and clubs to capture a man who had taught his followers to love their enemies. In response, Jesus simply submitted. He made no attempt to escape, and he stopped his disciples from defending him. "Put your sword back in its place . . . for all who draw the sword will die by the sword" (Matthew 26:52).

All Jesus' disciples ran into the darkness. Not one stayed to support him or to share the burden of mistreatment. I cannot blame them for running, but the impact on Jesus was severe. The rest of that terrible day, he would be without support or friendship.

Those who would follow Jesus' steps must face this squarely. When you are mistreated and deserted, you will not rage in defiance and bitterness, nor strike out at your tormentors. You will tell your defenders to put up their swords.

In a very small way I had to do that this week. At the invitation of the editors of my local newspaper, I had published an article about Christmas. A week later the newspaper ran a letter from a fellow Christian attacking what I had said. Immediately I composed in my head a letter of response, superficially gracious but in reality cutting the legs out from under my opponent and making him look foolish. But I did not send the letter. I reflected on Jesus' example and knew that he would have said not a word. I put up my sword.

I am fully aware what an insignificant event that was. Yet still it cost me. If we want to follow Jesus' steps we will have to respond gently—or not respond at all—to far more bruising attacks in far more volatile situations.

INTERROGATION AND TRIAL

"Then some began to spit at him; they blindfolded him, struck him with their fists, and said, 'Prophesy!' And the guards took him and beat him" (Mark 14:65).

Jesus' trial had a predetermined result. The religious leaders, needing some kind of moral cover, produced witnesses and made a show of examining them. When that failed to get results, they questioned Jesus directly. It had the character of an interrogation, not an examination. They sought only one kind of answer. They would beat, berate and browbeat him until they heard incriminating words.

In answer Jesus said very little. He made no attempt to defend himself or to refute false testimony. His silence unnerved his accusers. "'Are you not going to answer? What is this testimony that these men are bringing against you?' But Jesus remained silent" (Matthew 26:62-63).

When he was dragged before Pilate, the Roman governor, Jesus continued his tenacious refusal to speak. "But Jesus made no reply, not even to a single charge—to the great amazement of the governor" (Matthew 27:14).

"The soldiers . . . put a purple robe on him, then twisted together a crown of thorns and set it on him. And they began to call out to him, 'Hail, king of the Jews!' Again and again they struck him on the head with a staff and spit on him. Falling on their knees, they paid homage to him" (Mark 15:16-19).

Abused, beaten, mocked, scorned, Jesus never retaliated or lashed out. The words of the slave spiritual are very apt: "He never said a mumbling word." (The slaves who first sang that surely knew about suffering unjustly and took Jesus as a model.)

Beginning in the darkness of night and continuing into midday, his tormentors dragged Jesus from one hostile courtroom to another. Strangers found amusement in taunting him. Yet in the plain, unadorned description of the Gospels, Jesus stood straight and calm, never wavering, begging, crying or shouting.

Jesus' attitude might be mistaken for stoicism. From the cross, however, he showed a different motive. "Father, forgive them, for they do not know what they are doing" (Luke 23:34). Jesus loved his tormentors, even as they determined to mock, torture and kill him.

A few days ago I stood in line at an airport terminal. I was putting my son on a flight for South Africa, where he would spend the summer doing research. The flight was overbooked and we were near the end of the line, which moved very slowly. It gradually became clear that several people would be bumped from the flight. There was, however, some question as to who. A young girl and her father had connecting flights in London going on to India. Would my son yield to them? The airline supervisor asked him. He thought a moment and said he would.

But then another couple began to protest: they too had connecting flights, and they had been in line ahead of the girl and her father. My son was asked again: would he yield to this second couple? The tone of the discussion turned sharp and grasping. Everyone in line felt they were unjustly suffering, and the general response was clearly not gracious or dominated by love. Rather, the patient, stoical attitude of waiting in line changed instantly to barely disguised hostility and self-defense. (My son, I am glad to say, acted gently and generously.)

You know how these reactions go. They are the same reactions you see when a bus runs late, when long lines form for bathrooms, when a teacher fails half the class with a test that nobody saw coming. Consider those petty matters and compare them to what Jesus went through with perfect gentleness. That is part of walking in Jesus' steps when trouble comes and we suffer unjustly. Rather than fighting for our rights, we should follow Jesus and respond in generosity and love.

FORSAKEN AND CRUCIFIED

Then they took Jesus out of the city to kill him. Crucifixion was a form of torture developed and sanctioned by the civilization supposed to be the most developed of its time. Crucifixion's only purpose was to demonstrate Roman cruelty and therefore create fear in subject peoples. Crucifixion was a slow death and a very public death. Jesus was tormented like an exhibit at the county fair, on display for the curious and the vengeful.

"Those who passed by hurled insults at him, shaking their heads" (Matthew 27:39). "In the same way the chief priests, the teachers of the law and the elders mocked him. 'He saved others,' they said, 'but he can't save himself! He's the King of Israel! Let him come down now from the cross, and we will believe in him. He trusts in God. Let God rescue him now if he wants him, for he said, "I am the Son of God."' In the same way the robbers who were crucified with him also heaped insults on him" (Matthew 27:41-44).

More than that: God left Jesus to die. "My God, my God, why have you forsaken me?" (Matthew 27:46).

It is important to understand this correctly. Jesus made this cry in

agony, but not in despair. He was praying a line of a psalm—the first
line of Psalm 22. That in itself was an act of faith. When you pray the
psalms you automatically join with the community of faith that wrote
these prayers and has prayed them for a thousand years.

I think it very likely that Jesus had been thinking of Psalm 22 all
day long. So much of the psalm tells of what seems to be an execution. So much of the psalm was echoed in Jesus' experience of that
day.

> All who see me mock me;
>> they hurt insults, shaking their heads:
> "He trusts in the LORD;
>> let the LORD rescue him.
> Let him deliver him,
>> since he delights in him." . . .
> Dogs have surrounded me;
>> a band of evil men has encircled me,
>> they have pierced my hands and my feet.
> I can count all my bones;
>> people stare and gloat over me.
> They divide my garments among them
>> and cast lots for my clothing. (Psalm 22:7-8, 16-18)

A STRANGE SONG

While the psalm speaks of Jesus' great anguish, it also suggests Jesus'
faith. Certainly Jesus knew the whole psalm. He knew how it ended.
In Psalm 22 the execution suddenly turns into salvation. When Jesus
prayed the psalm's first line, "My God, my God, why have you forsaken me?" he knew he would come to this: "Future generations will
be told about the Lord. They will proclaim his righteousness to a

people yet unborn—for he has done it" (Psalm 22:30-31).

To walk in Jesus' steps we must pray sincerely the desperation of the forsaken. Yet we pray this from within the tradition of God's people, who have always offered such despair before God. The Bible's prayers (unlike the relentlessly upbeat songs and prayers we usually pray in church) have plenty of unrelieved suffering and distress. They express emotion freely—all kinds of emotion, even horrific and blood-curdling emotion. Yet grief is always closely hemmed in by hope and miracle. And grief is always prayed from within the praying community of faith. We need to pray the psalms, as Jesus did.

We can easily fall off on one side or the other, into emotions of sheer darkness or untempered joy. Either one is ultimately inhuman. We cannot live with unrelieved depression and despair, nor can we endure the cheerful soul who chirps endlessly about the value of suffering. We need the honest portrayal of pain seen to its depths but expressed within a community of hope. The psalms give us that. So did Jesus.

THE FORGIVING WIDOW

Gladys Staines has become the best-known Christian in India after Mother Teresa. She and her husband, Graham—both from Australia—worked quietly for decades among leprosy victims. Faith became increasingly politicized in India, however, and in 1999 an anti-Christian mob set upon Graham's car while he and his two young sons were sleeping in it, parked outside a church. The mob doused the car with fuel and set it on fire, then prevented the Staineses from escaping. All three perished in the flames.

During the trial and conviction of a charismatic Hindu activist who led the mob, Graham was accused of provoking local outrage by converting hundreds of poor Indians. His leprosy mission was said to be a front for evangelism—an offense to devout Hindus. Neverthe-less, public opinion was sympathetic to the Staineses, especially when Gladys said that she intended to remain in India and continue her husband's work. She said that she forgave his killers. That one phrase—"I forgive them"—made the front pages of newspapers all over India.

On the fifth anniversary of Graham's death I happened to hear Gla-dys speak to morning chapel at Bangalore's Southern Asia Bible Col-lege (SABC). She is a tall, middle-aged woman, by no means a char-ismatic figure. Speaking slowly and hesitantly to the 250 Indian students who attend this Assemblies of God training institution, she recalled events leading up to her husband's murder. Just weeks be-fore, she had read in the news about anti-Christian riots in the state of Gujarat, where dozens of churches were burned. "I said, a little blasé, 'Well, Christians also need to forgive.' I little thought that ten days later, I would need to do so."

"We have to forgive," she told the students. "Jesus taught us to for-give."

Ivan Satyavrata, president of SABC, is a wiry man with an expres-sively melancholy face. "We always get asked," he said in closing the meeting, "why India has not turned to Christ. We all know the an-swer."

He paraphrased something Mahatma Gandhi once said: "I would like to become a Christian, if I could find one."

"Christians have been looked at as people who make tall claims about Christ," Satyavrata went on. "There have been many sermons preached, thousands of rupees invested. But 'forgive' is the shortest, most eloquent, most powerful sermon India has ever heard. It has done something for the church that our sister, through her pain, through her tears, did what Jesus would do. I don't think it is an accident that after that event, we have seen unprecedented numbers of people turning to Christ."

Looking slowly over the crowd of ardent young people gathered in SABC's chapel, Satyavrata concluded, "Some standing here may be called on to pay the same price."

DYING WE LIVE

And then Jesus died. He stopped breathing. His blood coagulated in his brain. His body cooled and stiffened. He was pulled down from the cross a flopping hunk of meat and bone. They wrapped his body in a cloth and put it in the ground. It was all over. His campaign had led to this: a corpse.

He lived the literal meaning of what he had taught his followers: "Unless a kernel of wheat falls to the ground and dies, it remains only a single seed. But if it dies, it produces many seeds. The man who loves his life will lose it" (John 12:24-25).

Charles Wesley's great hymn captures the emotion of such sacrifice: "Amazing love, how can it be, that thou my God shouldst die for me." We would never feel such astonished love for a Great Moral Teacher. Awe, yes. Respect, certainly. But not the tear-streaked, speechless love that the cross calls out. Jesus gave his life for his people. He gave it in the most dreadful circumstances—as a circus sideshow for the curious and the vengeful. Yet his example in doing so left an indelible imprint on his followers, some of whom would soon walk in these steps, too.

Out of his dead body would grow the lively body of Christ.

15

THE RISEN LORD

THE GOSPEL ACCOUNTS SAY JESUS died on a Friday, executed by Roman soldiers near Jerusalem. On Sunday he was walking around again, a living, breathing human being. People found this hard to believe at the time, and they still do.

Quite naturally, people have tried to read Jesus' resurrection as something else—a vision or a metaphor. We have never seen anything like resurrection apart from this one case. People try to fit unprecedented events into a familiar package.

The attempt makes hash of the actual testimony, however. N. T. Wright has argued convincingly that the Gospel accounts cannot be talking about a visionary encounter that inspired Jesus' traumatized disciples, nor do they use resurrection as a metaphor for newfound hope in the face of death and despair. The witnesses to Jesus' resurrection describe a fully alive, fully physical human being, somebody who died and is now alive again.

The important question is, so what? What does a risen man two thousand years ago have to do with us? For that matter, what did he mean for people in his own day? He was alive again; so what?

Another way to put the question is: was Jesus right about the kingdom of God? Throughout his ministry he announced that all God's promises to Israel were about to come true. Did they?

The average resident of Jerusalem might be pardoned for not immediately seeing it. Israel remained poor and oppressed. Roman soldiers still occupied the city. (Within forty years they would level it.) And yet the earliest Christian documents show Jesus' followers celebrating the resurrection as proof that he was right. They did not merely assert it, they jubilantly shouted it, as though it spoke for itself.

We get a weird dual reality. For most people in Jerusalem, Easter Sunday was just like any other first day of the week. The weeks and months that followed showed no sign of transformation. Yet in the same dull streets where most people went about their business, a small set of people claimed that something stupendous had happened. According to them, the world would never be the same.

They believed this on Jesus' authority. When he gave final directions to his disciples, he began with a simple, grand assertion: "All authority in heaven and on earth has been given to me" (Matthew 28:18). Think about that statement. If he had said, "All authority in Jerusalem has been given to me," it would have been an extraordinary claim. The chief priest or Pilate or any of the Roman centurions had a different idea about who held authority in Jerusalem. Yet Jesus claimed more than Jerusalem. He claimed authority in heaven and on earth. He proclaimed himself bigger than Augustus Caesar. He claimed to be the Messiah at the end of all things, to whom God brought the kings of the nations to "kiss the Son, lest he be angry and you be destroyed in your way" (Psalm 2:12).

The disciples, trying to understand such extravagant claims, asked, "Lord, are you at this time going to restore the kingdom to

Israel?" (Acts 1:6). As Andrew Walls notes, "No doubt the words . . . betray an inadequate understanding of [Jesus'] person and work. Nevertheless, he does not reject that understanding as altogether misplaced. He does not say, 'I am not in the business of giving the Kingdom back to Israel, you should keep out of politics and concentrate on inner spiritual qualities.' He accepts . . . the question in the terms in which [it is] posed. . . . 'It is not for you to know when.'"

By the time Peter preached his first sermon, his questions were replaced by triumphant confidence. "God has made this Jesus, whom you crucified, both Lord and Christ" (Acts 2:36). Peter says that by raising Jesus from the dead, God has established him as the ruler who brings all God's promises to fulfillment.

By his second sermon, Peter was explaining a miraculous healing as absolutely typical of what one would expect in this new era. "Why does this surprise you? . . . The God of Abraham, Isaac and Jacob, the God of our fathers, has glorified his servant Jesus" (Acts 3:12-13). Peter explained that the risen Jesus had the power to forgive Israel's sins and fulfill Israel's story. "Repent, then, and turn to God, so that your sins may be wiped out, that times of refreshing may come from the Lord, and that he may send the Christ, who has been appointed for you—even Jesus. He must remain in heaven until the time comes for God to restore everything, as he promised long ago through his holy prophets" (Acts 3:19-21). "Indeed, all the prophets from Samuel on, as many as have spoken, have foretold these days. And you are heirs of the prophets and of the covenant God made with your fathers. He said to Abraham, 'Through your offspring all peoples on earth will be blessed'" (Acts 3:24-25).

The question remains: how did Jesus' resurrection accomplish such blessing? Peter preached as though everything had changed and all Israel's promises had been fulfilled, but how so? One cripple was healed, but a great many others remained begging on Jerusalem's streets. One man was raised from the dead, but many others remained corpses. Why did Peter sound so sure that Israel's grand and tragic story was wrapping up with a happy ending?

The dilemma is just as real today. Christians claim that Jesus was the most significant figure in the history of the world. Yet history goes on, apparently indifferent. Wars, disease and prejudice still plague us; money and might rule our everyday lives. What difference did Jesus make? Who cares if he rose again?

How Resurrection Spoke, and What It Said

Jesus' resurrection did not strike the disciples out of the blue. They already had well-formed ideas about resurrection, as did all Jews in first-century Jerusalem. The topic was so important that different groups of Jews were identified by their belief (or disbelief) in it, so much so that some had tried to draw Jesus into their controversies (Matthew 22:23-33). Years later Paul deliberately stirred up the same debates in a courtroom setting, confident that he could set off a red-hot argument (Acts 23:6-8). These controversies had nothing to do with Eastern myths about gods dying and coming back to life. In Jewish thinking, resurrection had to do with human beings, not gods.

Relatively speaking, resurrection was a new concept—only a few hundred years old. Through most of their history Jews had vague ideas about life after death, not startlingly different from what many other peoples of their period believed. The dead survived, they thought, but only in the shadowy netherworld called Sheol, where they dwelt helplessly in darkness and silence.

"No one remembers you when he is dead.
    Who praises you from Sheol?" (Psalm 6:5)

Unlike, say, the Egyptians, Jews showed little curiosity about this shadowy afterlife. Some cultures and religions, then as now, speculated about the preexistence of the soul, its survival after death, the possibility of communication with the dead, reincarnation and other such matters. In general Jews were uninterested. The simple reason was their robust appreciation for creation. God had made the world full of living, breathing creatures. Creation was good, very good. Life was lived here in physical existence. "Let everything that has breath praise the LORD" (Psalm 150:6).

In some ways their orientation was strikingly modern. Old Testament Jews took great pleasure in family, nature, possessions, agriculture. They counted their wealth in tangible things. Jews knew nothing of a soul's existence before birth, and they cared little for a shadowy spirit existence after death. They only knew that death ended the wonderful life of a created person on the earth.

We can identify with them in that. Spirituality may be wonderful, but how can it compare with rock climbing? Dancing? Kissing? The delights of life are irrepressibly physical. Who wants to die and lose all that? How could spiritual survival compensate, even in the slightest?

During the great, grievous tragedy of the exile, the prophet Ezekiel introduced the idea of resurrection as a metaphor. Ezekiel's vision (Ezekiel 37) showed exiled Israel as utterly dead—bleached bones scattered on a valley floor. "Son of man, can these bones live?" (Ezekiel 37:3). I daresay few who chant, "The knee bone's connected to the thigh bone" realize that they are singing an ancient Jewish portrait of hope in the face of national devastation. Ezekiel watched as the bones came together. Flesh and tendon grew to link them, skin covered them and finally the corpses began to breathe. "They came to life and stood up on their feet—a vast army" (Ezekiel 37:10).

This is a metaphor for Israel's recovery from a disastrous exile.

Israel would rise again. Flesh! Bone! Breath! God means a real recovery, not some spiritual triumph.

Then, in a startling innovation, the book of Daniel turned this metaphor into concrete reality. "There will be a time of distress such as has not happened from the beginning of nations until then. But at that time your people—everyone whose name is found written in the book—will be delivered. Multitudes who sleep in the dust of the earth will awake: some to everlasting life, others to shame and everlasting contempt" (Daniel 12:1-2).

In other words, God would redeem Israel from her distress not only by restoring future generations to the land but by reviving all Israel—including those who "sleep" in the dust. Sheol would be emptied. The resurrection would bring everyone back to life—some to everlasting life, some to contempt. Thus did the hope of resurrection begin in Israel.

It developed into a steady opinion. The Maccabean martyrs testified to their belief in it when tortured:

> After the first brother had died [by being scalped, his hands and feet cut off, and then being thrown into a red-hot pan], the soldiers started amusing themselves with the second one by tearing the hair and skin from his head. Then they asked him, "Now will you eat this pork, or do you want us to chop off your hands and feet one by one?"
>
> He replied in his native language, "I will never eat it!" So the soldiers tortured him, just as they had the first one, but with his dying breath he cried out to the king, "You butcher! You may kill us, but the King of the universe will raise us from the dead and give us eternal life, because we have obeyed his laws."
>
> The soldiers began entertaining themselves with the third

brother. When he was ordered to stick out his tongue, he quickly did so. Then he bravely held out his hands and courageously said, "God gave these to me. But his laws mean more to me than my hands, and I know God will give them back to me again." The king and those with him were amazed at his courage and at his willingness to suffer.

After he had died, the soldiers tortured the fourth one in the same cruel way, but his final words were, "I am glad to die at your hands, because we have the assurance that God will raise us from death. But there will be no resurrection to life for you, Antiochus!" (2 Maccabees 7:7-14)

These martyred brothers, heroes to subsequent generations of Jews, took courage from the resurrection. They anticipated a restored bodily life, not reincarnation or "afterlife." An individual's very hands would be given back when God redeemed his people.

Though hope in resurrection was a distinctly Jewish belief, not all Jews believed in it. The New Testament specifies that the Sadducees did not. The Pharisees, who disagreed with Jesus on many issues, agreed with him about the resurrection. According to N. T. Wright, the majority of Jews had developed a strong expectation of resurrection. Jesus agreed with them unconditionally, and he sharply corrected those who did not (see Mark 12:18-27).

This belief in resurrection was not, strictly speaking, a belief in afterlife. It was belief in life-after-afterlife. If dead people were to be resurrected, it stood to reason they must survive somehow in the interim—if only as a "spirit" or a "soul." In that respect resurrectionists carried on the earlier Jewish belief, common with other religions, that the person survived even when his or her body was dead. They found very little in that to interest them, however. They wanted real life, bone-and-breath life. They wanted to see all Israel brimming with life that would never die.

They did not think of resurrection as a gift they would inherit individually. Resurrection was for Israel. It would be the grand revival of their nation, when all her great hopes would be fulfilled. Her sins would be forgiven, she would fill the Promised Land, her enemies would be shattered, God would once again live in intimate and loving fellowship with his people, and all God's people beginning with Abraham would be resurrected to live together in peace and joy. Jesus referred to this general resurrection when he predicted that "many will come from the east and the west, and will take their places at the feast with Abraham, Isaac and Jacob in the kingdom of heaven" (Matthew 8:11). In announcing that the kingdom was at hand, Jesus might have added, "and the resurrection with it."

People sometimes unthinkingly merge resurrection with Egyptian or Greek ideas about the afterlife, but they are quite different. Greek Platonism, for example, taught that spiritual realities were deeper and more permanent than physical life. We should not, therefore, become too enamored with brief earthly pleasures. Our bodies will die and decay, but the eternal soul will live on. Knowing about the afterlife makes Platonists less attached to the here and now.

The Jews' hope for resurrection had just the opposite effect. It made people even more attached to bodily life, for it said that flesh and blood would carry on into eternity.

WHY RESURRECTION MATTERS TO ME

This view of resurrection is not a quaint theological oddity. It has deep, emotional consequences. Let me illustrate with my own family story.

At the age of eleven my father lost his father. It was during the

Depression, and my grandfather had already been unemployed for some time when he succumbed to cancer. Left with nothing, my grandmother took her two boys all the way from Syracuse, New York, to San Francisco, where she had a sister. They bravely cobbled together a living on the city streets, moving frequently from one house to another.

During high school my dad became a Christian, which utterly changed his outlook. That plus the GI Bill motivated him to go to college and seminary after serving in World War II. He married, became a pastor and raised a family. Like many Depression-era kids, he made a success of his life. However, I don't know that he ever completely got over his father's death. He grew up as a lonely soul, prone to occasional depression. He missed something growing up without a dad.

What if God had allowed him a spiritual sense of his father, alive in heaven? People go to séances seeking just that. If such a spiritual visit were possible, would it have helped? I imagine my father as a teenager coming home from selling newspapers on the tough streets of San Francisco. Just as he enters the apartment he experiences a spiritual encounter. Perhaps he feels his father's presence in the room and receives a telepathic message that his father loves him very much. Perhaps he comes to believe that his father is in heaven watching over him.

Such a spiritual encounter might have helped, but how much? Not enough to transform the life of a lonely, struggling teenager. My dad needed a father in flesh and blood. He needed a dad to work with him, fixing the car or planting the garden. He needed a father to go for a ride in the truck. He needed a father to play catch on the street. Nothing but a fully resurrected father could fill the hole in my father's life.

What a terrible thief is death. What awful destruction it did in my father's life, taking away his dad. Death insults and destroys the full, articulated beauty of God's created life. Death is our enemy, for it annihilates the people we love.

Now my father is in his eighties, suffering from Alzheimer's. He paces from room to room, unable to remember where he is. For the past five years I have watched him dying by the centimeter. One by one the lights in his face wink out. He was a passionate, intelligent, lively human being. He always came into a room with some burning thought to share, some passion he felt compelled to tell you about— a piece of music, a book he had read, a photograph he had taken or a flower he had seen. Those outsized passions have faded out. He generally stares, heavily and lifelessly. I hate the thief death, who is brazenly stealing my dad away.

I don't want a soul survival. I want my living, breathing, talking dad. Only resurrection can give me back my dad.

THE FIRST OF MANY

Hope for that kind of resurrection was in the background when Jesus unexpectedly came back from the dead. His resurrection gave his followers a huge jolt. All the accounts show that they were not expecting it. What did it mean? Given their expectations for resurrection, they had to see it as hugely, if strangely, significant. No Jew could evaluate Jesus' return to life as a random, one-off miracle. Surely it happened as part of the bigger picture—the whole story of Israel and the kingdom of God.

Jesus' resurrection was clearly not "the resurrection." That applied to "everyone whose name is found written in the book . . . multitudes who sleep in the dust of the earth" (Daniel 12:1-2). Nothing like the general resurrection happened when Jesus rose from the dead. He was alive again, but the rest of the dead remained decaying in their tombs. Something dramatic had happened, but what?

It must have been difficult to make sense of. Nothing in Jewish thinking spoke of a resurrected Messiah. Nobody was prepared for a single, as opposed to a general, resurrection—not even the disciples, who had heard Jesus predict it.

And yet it made sense that the Messiah should lead the way for all Israel. Just as David fought Goliath as Israel's representative, so the new anointed king would stand in Israel's place to battle death. His victories would lead the way for the whole nation.

Seeing that Jesus had risen from the dead, and that nobody else had, Jesus' disciples concluded that resurrection is a two-step process. Step one: Jesus. Step two: everybody else.

One thing is for sure: the resurrection was an extraordinary vindication of Jesus' claims. If anybody else were to rise from the dead— Peter, say, or John the Baptist—that would certainly not prove him to be the Son of God, the Messiah. In such cases resurrection would be amazing and intriguing, but it would be subject to multiple interpretations and speculations. It would prove nothing.

In Jesus' case, resurrection came as a direct contradiction of what his tormentors had said about him. He had been executed for claiming God's anointing to lead Israel—for leading the people astray. They killed him to prove his claims nonsense, and they mocked him for it. "He trusts in God. Let God rescue him now if he wants him, for he said, 'I am the Son of God'" (Matthew 27:43). "Let this Christ, this King of Israel, come down now from the cross, that we may see and believe" (Mark 15:32). Such were the taunts Jesus heard at his execution.

Many men in that era believed themselves chosen by God to lead Israel against her enemies. Most of them ended up dead, and that was the end of that. "A messiah who was executed . . . was not, after all, the true Messiah," N. T. Wright puts it. Jesus' death clearly proved that his critics were right: God had not chosen him.

Sometimes I hear people criticize the disciples' dispirited response to Jesus' crucifixion. They scattered. Well, of course! Why follow a dead Messiah? Death has a tendency to be final. But when Jesus came to life again, it reversed that judgment. He really was God's Messiah. Through the resurrection God set his seal of approval on Jesus.

If Jesus was God's anointed leader, then the blessings he experienced should flow, sooner or later, to his people. So Israel understood kings. Their glory, their triumphs would be the nation's glory and triumph. Whatever happened to Jesus should ultimately pass on as a gift to his people. That's how Paul saw it when he wrote to the Corinthians, who had come to doubt their own resurrection. (Perhaps they merely expected soul survival, or "heaven.") Paul made clear that Jesus' resurrection is closely linked to our resurrection. "If the dead are not raised, then Christ has not been raised either. And if Christ has not been raised, your faith is futile; you are still in your sins" (1 Corinthians 15:16-17). The point is so important that Paul repeats himself, almost word for word—something he almost never does. When we see the risen Jesus, Paul suggests, we are seeing our future. "Just as we have borne the likeness of the earthly man [Adam], so shall we bear the likeness of the man from heaven [Jesus]" (1 Corinthians 15:49).

Paul makes the same point in the magnificent crescendo of Romans 8: "For those God foreknew he also predestined to be conformed to the likeness of his Son, that he might be the firstborn among many brothers" (Romans 8:29).

Here is how Eugene Peterson paraphrases it in *The Message:* "[God] decided from the outset to shape the lives of those who love him along the same lines as the life of his Son. The Son stands first in the line of humanity he restored. We see the original and intended shape of our lives there in him."

Jesus' resurrection is the first installment of total resurrection. Thus it matters tremendously whether Jesus actually came back to bodily life, as opposed to a spirit-Jesus. Those who love the creation want to live as the creation. We are body-persons—always have been, always will be. Jesus' resurrection leads the way for body life eternally. The tide has turned. The victory is won. The wonderful creation will be cleansed and completed, with pain and death wiped away.

THE SALK POLIO VACCINE

N. T. Wright points out that at least one first-century rebel, when he had won a few battles, had coins minted with the year "1." The way he saw it, a new era had begun, even if some details were yet to be worked out. So with Jesus: the decisive battle was won when he died and rose again. The kingdom had come. Sins were forgiven, the barrier between God and his people was broken, a renewed people of God was identified, a down payment of healing and love was being distributed, and in principle the old enemy, death, was eliminated. You can start celebrating now.

I like to compare it to the Salk polio vaccine. Through much of the twentieth century, polio was a fearsome killer. It particularly attacked children, who often died a cruelly slow death as paralysis took away their ability to move and finally to breathe. Epidemics swept across populations, killing randomly. All medical efforts proved fruitless.

Historian Jane Smith writes that in the 1930s two American medical researchers, Maurice Brodie and John Kollmer, separately developed vaccines that they tried first on monkeys, then on humans. Neither succeeded, and Kollmer's vaccine tragically spread polio to many who tried it. "Gentlemen, this is one time I wish the floor would open up and swallow me," Kollmer reportedly said to a gathering of his colleagues. Chastened, other researchers pulled back.

Polio spread more rapidly during World War II, perhaps because of the vast movements of refugees and soldiers. The worst epidemics in American history struck after that war, reaching a peak during the early fifties—58,000 cases in 1952 alone.

Jonas Salk began work on polio in 1947. Being new to the field, he tried innovative techniques, which speeded his research. He went back to Maurice Brodie's approach, which involved isolating the polio virus and killing it using the chemical formalin. Early testing of such "killed virus" vaccines showed enough promise to justify a huge, two-million-child field trial in 1954. It was an outsized, expensive experiment, but the panic over polio justified the effort.

On April 12, 1955, results were announced in a press conference broadcast live on radio and television. The vaccine worked. Those vaccinated were half as likely to contract polio, and furthermore those who did catch polio were less likely to become severely paralyzed. The response was euphoria. "Flushed by the first report that the vaccine had worked," Smith writes, "exuberant citizens rushed to ring church bells and fire sirens, shouted, clapped, sang and made every kind of joyous noise they could. City councils and state legislatures postponed their regular business to draft resolutions congratulating Salk for his wonderful achievement."

In reality, polio continued to hurt people. It took two years to make enough vaccine for all Americans. Even by 1970—fifteen years after the discovery—only about seventy percent of Americans under age twenty had been vaccinated. And that did not begin to touch the global problem.

An estimated 100,000 cases were reported worldwide in 1993, and polio came back in countries where it had once been eliminated. Polio is a stubborn survivor, even today when the tools for its eradication are widely available.

What did America celebrate with such giddy excitement on April 12, 1955? The simplest and truest answer is that they celebrated the defeat of polio.

Were they correct to celebrate in 1955, seeing that polio would continue to exist and to kill for an indefinite time? Only a spoilsport could tell them no. Theirs was one of the great triumphs of the era. It would benefit untold millions yet to be born. Surely great celebration was in order!

The first generation of Christians celebrated Jesus' resurrection. They experienced the firstfruits of the kingdom. Death was defeated. Perhaps they would have been sobered to know that thousands of years would pass with this vanquished killer still vital, still deadly. Nevertheless the triumph they felt was real. Death, where is your victory? Grave, where is your sting? In Jesus' resurrection God had demonstrated the destruction of our great enemy.

Do You Believe like Jesus?

I am afraid that a lot of what passes for Christian teaching about life after death would receive the same rebuke that Jesus gave the Sadducees: "You are badly mistaken!" (Mark 12:27). A popular version of the gospel is: God forgives our sins so that we can go to heaven when we die. Heaven is conceived of as a place that has no geography, no soil, no material wealth. Our loved ones are there, but they float in a vague, spiritual glow—they don't do anything, nor do they have anything to talk about (except what we do on earth, which they evidently spend much of their time watching). There is more Plato than Bible in this view.

"Just a few more weary days and then, I'll fly away." That is how a popular gospel tune puts it. In popular doctrine, heaven is the end of the line. Once we get there, we are done. Our years of earthly toil and struggle won't seem so important.

Biblically, however, the heaven we enter at death is not the end of the line. As Peter said of Jesus in his second sermon, "He must remain in heaven *until the time comes for God to restore everything*, as he promised long ago through his holy prophets" (Acts 3:21, emphasis added). What happens after death unfolds in two stages. The first is an interim state called heaven. We know little about it, though it is a place of comfort where we will be "with Christ" until the resurrection (Philippians 1:23). But then, in the resurrection, heaven comes to earth and we all come fully to life again. That is our great hope.

Resurrection is living, breathing life. Scripture speaks of a new heaven and a new earth, and of a new city lit by the presence of God. We will enjoy, I presume, what we enjoy now, only more so. Laughter, silliness, masculinity, femininity, music, sports, food, drink and certainly worship—there is no point in carrying on the list. What do you love? It has a future when the world is made right.

Jesus loved the world that God had made—and especially he loved its living creatures. He did not live like someone with one foot in the spirit world. He loved people of all kinds, and he went to all kinds of parties. People who believe in resurrection are like that—they love God's creation and relish life in the body.

THINK OF THE BENEFITS

The first generation of Christians had not yet experienced the promised total resurrection. Yet so much good had come to them, they had to celebrate.

- *They had seen the Messiah.* For so long—for centuries—God's people had peered into the dim future, hoping to recognize God's rescuing king. "Concerning this salvation, the prophets . . . searched intently and with the greatest care, trying to find out the time and circumstances to which the Spirit of Christ in them was pointing when he predicted the sufferings of Christ and the glories that would follow. . . . Even angels long to look into these things" (1 Peter 1:10-12). Now the believers were convinced they held the long-awaited secret. They had seen the Messiah, he had been publicly vindicated by God, and they belonged to his movement.

- *A renewed people were chosen.* A "remnant" was taken from old, discouraged Israel. These people had a new heart to obey God through God's Spirit.

- *Sins were forgiven.* Their separation from God had been obliterated. God had returned to his people, having accepted the Messiah's once-for-all sacrifice for sin on their behalf. They had peace with God.

- *The nations were coming to join them in worship.* God's renewed people were becoming a gathering point for the peoples of the world, just as the prophets had said.

- *God's blessings were spreading.* Some were healed. Some spoke in new languages or prophesied. A new Spirit animated them as they gathered. They experienced great comfort from God and from each other as they lived in a renewed community that worshiped God. Life made sense. They knew where God was taking them.

- *Their enemies were defeated.* Suddenly the Romans (or Greeks or Syrians or Egyptians) were not enemies at all. Instead, death and sin were seen clearly as the real enemies. Jesus had broken these powers at his resurrection. They remained dangerous, but only for the interim until God would restore his entire creation, so long spoiled by death and destruction.

Such were the immediate benefits of Jesus' resurrection. We enjoy them today. May we never take them for granted!

The early Christians knew that Jesus was vindicated in what he had proclaimed: the kingdom had come. As Paul wrote, they were those on whom "the fulfillment of the ages has come" (1 Corinthians 10:11). Yet they also knew that they must wait, watch and worship, crying out repeatedly, "Come, Lord Jesus!"

The Christian believer has both feet in God's kingdom. "If anyone is in Christ, he is a new creation; the old has gone, the new has come!" (2 Corinthians 5:17). "Now is the time of God's favor, now is the day of salvation" (2 Corinthians 6:2).

16

RESURRECTION LIFE

WE HAVE NOW REACHED THE END OF Jesus' life on earth. He ascended into heaven and has stayed there. A new era has begun in which the impact of Jesus' life is felt, though he is not here in the flesh. He has left his followers to do his work, led by his Holy Spirit.

A bad exchange, one would think! Him for us? What was he thinking?

There was sense to it, though. The movement had focused around one man who could be present at only one place at a time. Amazing as Jesus was, he was limited by culture and language. He spent his entire career in tiny Palestine, exposed to perhaps a few hundreds of thousands of people—mostly Jews. His followers at the end of his life numbered about a hundred and twenty (Acts 1:15). Today we are perhaps two billion, from every conceivable culture and nationality. The kingdom can be seen at work in towns and villages all over the world.

Jesus very deliberately started a movement. He knew what he was doing when he left us to carry on. He wanted to burst the boundaries of time, space and culture to transform the world. He is doing just exactly that, now, through us.

JESUS' AGENDA

Having closely examined the story of Jesus' life, we can now answer some basic questions. Just what was his agenda for A.D. 30? What is his agenda for today?

The answer to both questions can be simply answered: Jesus' agenda is the kingdom of God. In A.D. 30 Jesus led the way into the fulfillment of Israel's story. He created the breakthrough conditions that would enable a people to live in harmony with their king. Today his agenda is to guide the people who love him until at last God's people and God's rule cover everything.

Jesus' agenda has to do with a family living in love with the ruler of the earth. This is, of course, an agenda that began with Abraham, who was called by God in these famous words:

> I will make you into a great nation
>   and I will bless you;
> I will make your name great,
>   and you will be a blessing.
> I will bless those who bless you,
>   and whoever curses you I will curse;
> and all peoples on earth
>   will be blessed through you. (Genesis 12:2-3)

Jesus' agenda lived out this promise. He would make a great nation. A nation is not merely a collection of individuals; it is a people with a sense of their joint authority. Linked by a common identity, God's people take responsibility for their land—to work justice, to care for creation, above all to love and care for all God's creatures.

In Jesus' agenda the people of God would never be independent, but blessed by God they would rely on the one from whom all blessings flow. He would give them a great name. Not only would God's people be blessed, they would become a blessing. Their very nature and character would be transformed.

Those who bless you, God will bless. Those who curse you, God will curse. God's family need not punish or bribe; God will protect them and foster their relations with others so that in the end blessings flow through God's people to every last ethnic corner on the earth. The extent of God's kingdom is boundless; it will embrace all peoples. So God announced to Abraham. So Jesus announced and began. So we live.

One can scoff, of course. How much real power does this "kingdom" possess, compared to science and technology, compared to the forces of the marketplace, compared to the powers of governments, compared to the forces of nature? Only those with ears to hear and eyes to see will grasp that Jesus' agenda is moving forward and that nothing can stop it. Today we can see what Jesus' disciples hardly dreamed: that from a small group in a single upstairs room, his movement has spread to every corner of the earth.

We are—the church is—the answer to Jesus' prayers. He succeeded at his calling, and we are the result. Not as we are now, of course. I suppose the pride Jesus takes in us is like the pride of the parent of a teenager—five parts love, three parts hope, and one part realistic assessment. Jesus loves us for what he can see in us. From us, his body, will unfold the full flowering of the kingdom. He can see it already, just as he saw it in those Palestinian peasants who first followed him.

WATCHING GOD WORK

Social theorist Rene Girard makes an intriguing case that the gospel has a power independent of our efforts. According to his analysis, societies build themselves on ritualized violence against those they define as their enemies. Such "sacred violence" creates society's sense of power and legitimacy, Girard says. Think of the solemn rituals that accompany an execution, for example. (At one time executions were done publicly, for the "moral improvement of society.") Or consider the quasireligious feelings of Americans regarding the war on terror. Our solemnity and sanctimony suggest that we are doing more than protecting ourselves. Something holy is involved when we wreak vengeance on our enemies. War reconsecrates our nation.

Before Jesus, Girard says, such attitudes were instinctive and unashamed. National strong men were honored and admired. Without a hint of regret, conquering heroes built pyramids from their victims' skulls and crucified hundreds along well-built Roman highways.

Since Jesus, Girard claims, that society-building violence is increasingly undermined. The story of the cross has changed everything.

The gospel tells of a man who became a victim of the civil powers—and this victimized man we worship as Lord! Since Jesus, we increasingly join the side of those who suffer instead of respecting their oppressors. That has caused empires to break down because people feel sympathy for the conquered native. (Think of India and Gandhi.) Law and order crumble because we sympathize with the accused. (Think of the LA riots and Rodney King.) Executions can no longer be carried out publicly because the public cannot stand to see a victim suffer—not even a victim they believe to be guilty of horrific crimes. All this undermines the authority of traditional society.

Gil Bailie, one of Girard's interpreters, illustrates the trend this way. "There's plenty of truth in the revised picture of Western history that the young are now routinely taught, the picture of the West's swashbuckling appetite for power, wealth and dominion. What's to be

noted is that it is we, the spiritual beneficiaries of that less than always edifying history, who automatically empathize more with our
ancestors' victims than with our ancestors themselves."

Ever since Calvary, Girard says, our sympathy for the victim
grows. Every year it creates new contradictions for those who seek to
maintain order on the basis of coercion. As the story of the cross becomes known in wider and wider circles, it unleashes a dynamic with
deep and unpredictable implications for society.

Audacious and unproveable, Girard's analysis fascinates me because it suggests the gospel's independent power. The story of God's
Son on the cross sets in motion forces beyond human control.
Through such means God will bring his kingdom to fullness in a time
of his choosing and in ways that we cannot predict. It is not for us "to
know the times or dates the Father has set by his own authority"
(Acts 1:7).

Our Part to Play

Yet Jesus expected his disciples to do more than sit back and watch
the gospel work. He left them with instructions for ongoing action.
"As you sent me into the world," Jesus prayed, "I have sent them into
the world" (John 17:18). The disciples were told to "make disciples
of all nations" (Matthew 28:19). "You will be receive power when the
Holy Spirit comes on you; and you will be my witnesses in Jerusalem,
and in all Judea and Samaria, and to the ends of the earth" (Acts 1:8).

So it has happened. Throughout history Christians have been activists—monks, martyrs and missionaries, as well as farmers, entre-
preneurs and scientists. They have built societies that aim at justice,
filled with music, literature and science. Missionaries have gone fear-
lessly into the most difficult, God-rejecting places, learning new languages and adapting to alien cultures. Not everything they have done

is admirable. Sometimes activist Christians have done terrible things in the name of Christ. Nevertheless, doing far more good than bad, they have built a worldwide community of believers, its core documents (the Scriptures) translated into far more languages than any other document, its worship conducted in almost every nation on earth.

Church historian Andrew Walls says that Christianity spreads through translation. He means translation between cultures as well as between languages. The gospel began in the culture and language of Israel, was soon translated into the languages of Greece and Rome, and thence into English and Gaelic and Russian. Paul, Augustine, Patrick, Francis, Luther, Edwards, Graham, Teresa: each translated the gospel in a new setting. As the translation goes on and spreads out around the world, we discover more and more hidden riches—new meanings and applications.

Translating is creative work. How do you translate "the house built on rock" in a land where there is no rock? How do you translate "bread and wine" in a culture that forbids alcohol? Translators must find words in the new language to translate such biblical terms as "glory," "salvation," "flesh" and even concrete images like "sheep and goats" and "vine and branches." The gospel takes the shape and color, even the taste, of the language and culture that receives it.

The result is a magnificent variety. There are vast differences between drum-beating Pentecostal worshipers in rural India and Baptists attending megachurches in Southern California. It does not follow that one is right and another wrong. Quite possibly both have accurately translated the life of Jesus into their circumstances.

It matters tremendously, however, that they know what they are translating. "I am the vine," Jesus said. "You are the branches. If a man remains in me and I in him, he will bear much fruit" (John

15:5). That verse is often understood in a mystical sense: through prayer we must stay connected to Jesus. It should also be understood in a historical sense. If we lose touch with who Jesus is and what he did as told us in the Scriptures, we will not bear good fruit. We are a historical movement. We must know where we came from in order to chart our direction.

The first generation of Christians understood how crucial this is. They carefully and faithfully recorded the story of Jesus' life. They also copied and passed on the Hebrew Scriptures that Jesus revered. We have this wealth of information about Jesus' life and his context so that we can understand his life and know how to follow his steps.

How the Maori Came to Faith

To illustrate how the gospel gets translated, Walls relates the story of the Maori, New Zealand's indigenous people. When Europeans first contacted them, the Maori were cannibals who delighted in ritualized warfare. They were happy with their way of life and felt no guilt for its violence and bloodshed.

Missionaries in the early nineteenth century met with little success. In eighteen years they made just two converts. The Maori "were not remotely interested in Christianity," Walls writes. "For twenty years of proclamation of the evangelical gospel there was only one unmistakable achievement: the missionaries had proved that it was possible to live with the Maori without being killed and eaten."

Even that dubious achievement had its dark side. Seeing that the missionaries survived, other Westerners moved in, selling guns. For the first time, the Maori saw a substantial benefit in Western civilization: better technology for making war.

However, within a fairly short time the firearms disenchanted even the Maori. Their code of honor insisted that they avenge killings.

Great shame came on anyone who failed to fight for the honor of his clan. The guns, though, were far too efficient. Battles that once killed a handful of warriors would now slaughter scores. Maori grew depressed as violence increased and they realized they might very well wipe each other out. But how could they stop fighting without losing honor? "They began to feel themselves trapped in a tyrannous circle of events they could no longer control." For the first time the Maori longed for peace, but they had no resources in themselves to achieve it. "The only way to get rid of self-destructive war was to give up the system under which it was conducted, and the only viable way of doing that was to take up a new way of life."

Maori began to convert in great numbers and to spread the "gospel of peace" from clan to clan. During the second eighteen years of missionary experience, the majority of the Maori became Christian, reading the Bible and forming congregations with real enthusiasm. Yet the missionaries were far from ecstatic about it, because it did not seem like "real" conversion to them.

For the missionaries, conversion to Christ had to do with conviction of sin and the sense of God's forgiveness. "Where was the mourning for sin, and the rejoicing in forgiveness, which should mark a real conversion?" Yet no one could miss seeing that God was at work. Indeed, classic marks of conversion were present. The Maori turned away from their former way of life and toward the God of the Bible. They took great risks in rejecting the spirits they had known since childhood and in turning the other cheek toward their enemies.

As Walls says, "The Maori responded to the gospel, not to the missionaries' experience of the gospel." They understood that the very Jesus who had commanded his followers to love their enemies had himself voluntarily died at the hands of his enemies, and that this event had "made the two one and . . . destroyed the barrier, the di-

viding wall of hostility" (Ephesians 2:14). It took great faith for the
Maori to leave the old way of life and enter another, finding peace—
public, historical peace. The Maori grasped how the gospel of Jesus
Christ spoke in the language of their own culture. They did the work
of translation.

The missionaries had felt the impact of the gospel in one way. It
liberated them from their sense of personal guilt and inner failure.
The Maori experienced the gospel in another way. They were freed
from actual warfare. These were not, as the missionaries feared, different faiths. They were the same faith, applied to different situations.
Both traced back directly to the good news that Jesus announced.

In Jesus' Steps

Scripture gives us no detailed plan for how to live the gospel in our
situation. We have to translate. We need creativity, inspiration and
careful analysis. Always, we start with Jesus' pattern and example. He
is the Word we translate.

In this book we have closely examined Jesus' life. We have tried to
understand just what he did in first-century Palestine, and why.
Frankly, his situation is very different from ours. His dealings with a
Roman occupation, with the Pharisees, with the temple and other
Jewish traditions are hard to compare to the twenty-first century.
Even the facts of disease that he faced as he sought to help people in
need are very different from today, with our hospitals and medical
procedures.

Even so, the New Testament consistently asserts that Jesus' life is
relevant as a pattern for ours. It is not simply background information, but an ongoing guide. We should not merely carry on Jesus'
mission, but do it in the same way that he did, following his steps. As
John wrote about life with God, "Whoever claims to live in him must

walk as Jesus did" (1 John 2:6). That is my point in this book. By looking carefully at Jesus' life, we learn how we are meant to live. In many ways his life directs and corrects ours.

- *Jesus was baptized.* In so doing, he accepted his identity as part of Israel, sins and all. So we begin our journey by being baptized and taking on our identity as part of God's family, the church. We are not alone. We do not operate in a vacuum. Rather we have roots that go thousands of years deep and a community that extends all over the globe. We do not define ourselves by our personal tastes and desires as individualists and consumerists do. Like Jesus, we define ourselves by our God-given community, God's people. We belong to them, and we serve them.

- *Jesus faced temptation.* Satan wanted him to "succeed" in a way that would lead him away from God's purposes. To overcome temptation Jesus relied on Scripture rather than his own brilliance and spirituality. Scripture taught Jesus to listen to God's direction, to worship God alone and to wait for God. That kind of patient reliance on Scripture and Spirit direction must be ours, too, lest we fall into the temptation to succeed in the wrong way. Christians who follow Jesus' steps will be known for their scriptural orientation, for their devotion to God alone and for their willingness to wait for God's direction. Creative and brilliant they may be, but these devout qualities of faith and trust in God will always undergird them.

- *Jesus proclaimed the good news.* He stated that God's kingdom was breaking in. He spoke boldly and wanted to spread the gospel as widely as possible. We too must be people who speak to others about what God is doing in and through Jesus. "Join us and see what God is doing," we say. Jesus' movement will be known for its joyful witness that God is alive and active in our world.

- **Jesus called disciples** and trained them in a rigorous way of life. We must make room for God to call people today, and we must train them for radical discipleship. We are a movement, not a club: we prepare people for action, and our expectations are high.

- **Jesus healed and helped** wherever he experienced needy people. He never did it for publicity, but simply because his nature was to help people when they asked for help. So we must unfailingly help those in need, praying for them and doing all that is in our power to relieve their suffering. God provides his power to do amazing wonders when we work and pray in the name of Jesus.

- **Jesus prayed.** He sought solitude to pray to God, and he taught his disciples how to pray. We must pray as Jesus did and follow his instructions by praying the kingdom, not merely our own personal and individual desires. God's people are known for prayer, kingdom prayer.

- **Jesus warned, especially against hypocrisy.** He did not warn pagans, but "insiders" like the Pharisees, who knew God's Word. We also must warn each other when we see hypocrisy or lack of sincerity. Those who follow Jesus will not be spotless, but they will take spots seriously. Genuine holiness will be their constant concern, as it was for Jesus.

- **Jesus went to Jerusalem**, knowing he would suffer and die. We too must go to our Jerusalems, where opposition will meet us. Jesus' movement will always be drawn to the most difficult places on earth.

- *Jesus gave his life for others*, and so should we. We do not sacrifice for the sins of the world, but we willingly die to ourselves in order for others to live. That is the core of Jesus' example—his willingness to serve even to the point of death, without bitterness or rancor. To be like Jesus requires sacrifice for others' sake.

If we give our lives, God will raise us up, as he did Jesus.

WHERE CAN I SEE RESURRECTION LIFE?

When you put all this together, you get the movement that Jesus gave his life to launch. He proclaimed that Israel's story was coming to its fulfillment, that all God's promises were coming true in the kingdom of God. We see that fulfillment in God's people through the world—those who follow in Jesus' steps.

We live in the in-between time, long after the first excitement of Jesus' breakthrough victory but before the final consummation of his triumph. We endure the same weird dual reality the disciples encountered that first Easter. Believing in resurrection life, we also live with unredeemed reality—the dull meanness of the everyday.

Someone may ask: where can I see resurrection life? If Jesus has really brought all God's promises to fulfillment, it ought to be visible in flesh and blood.

We always see resurrection life in Jesus. He remains the only perfect life, full of life. He himself said, "I am the resurrection and the life. He who believes in me will live" (John 11:25). As we read the Scriptures and interact with Jesus through the power of the Holy Spirit, we have real contact with resurrection life. We don't merely imitate Christ, we are one with Christ and we live in him and in his power. The daily experience of fellowship with God is real.

Besides that, godly lives foreshadow the power of the resurrection. I met Lesslie Newbigin, the great theologian and missionary, about a year before his death. His eyesight was all but gone, and he lived with his wife in an ordinary eldercare home that offered little privacy and no hint of luxury. To hear it from him, you would have thought that he lived in a palace and that his fellow residents were Oxford dons. He saw it all through the eyes of faith, living a resurrected life in a most unrenewed world.

Anyone can find such people. They live everywhere, many quite unknown and unheralded. In *Soul Survivor: How My Faith Survived the Church*, Philip Yancey describes the individuals who modeled faith for him and helped him survive crises of doubt. Every Christian should have such a list—people whose lives exemplify the gospel.

The third evidence of resurrection life is in Jesus' family—the church all over the world. Yes, we are flawed, but together we are also the body of Christ—the resurrected body. We are bigger than any individual, bigger than any nation or culture. We transcend East and West, North and South. We are a billion hands and feet, and untold love.

The church is an enormous fact brimming with life—resurrection life. How has this family grown from a single nomad's offspring into a vast, varied congregation in every nation and tongue?

My wife, Popie, and I listened to Stephen Ambrose's *D-Day* on a recent car trip. In spellbinding detail Ambrose chronicles the massive planning and preparation of the invasion of Normandy in the Second World War. Ambrose interviewed many soldiers who were there, and he offers their perspectives.

Often they experienced screwups. Cockamamied plans went predictably wrong. Bombs were dropped miles off target. Men landed at the wrong place at the wrong time and with the wrong equipment.

Many died tragically through their own fellow soldiers' mistakes. Landing craft got off course and stuck on sandbars. Some were destroyed by German artillery before they even reached the beach. Many men who reached shore could not find their unit, and those who did were often bereft of equipment to do the assignments they had trained for. Seen from the battlefront, the scene was confusion, blood and terror. Many officers were sure that the invasion had failed, for all they saw was calamity.

From above, however, the view was different. Pilots looking down saw wave after wave of ships and planes in magnificent array. The local scene might be chaos, but the greater outlook was filled with hope of final victory. As events would show, the view from above was the accurate perspective, offering far better clues to the truth than the view "close to the action."

So for us. The wider our view of the church, the more likely we will understand the resurrection life that has begun.

The church may often seem weak and foolish compared to a political faction, a skilled lobby or a well-organized nonprofit organization. Jesus' church, however, demonstrates qualities they cannot touch, such as worship, proclamation of the gospel of peace and sacrificial love. Our strength lies in doing what is valuable in Jesus' sight. Our glory will be revealed on the day of the Lord Jesus.

JESUS' CHURCH

We who follow Jesus are tangible evidence of the kingdom come. We are a movement that Jesus carefully constructed, shaping it from his own family of historical Judaism. This is no mushroom, popping up on the fringes of culture. It is more like a redwood tree, growing from a sliver of green into something rooted and massive and full of life.

"God loves you and has a wonderful plan for your life." That is a great truth, but it makes up only a small slice of the greater good news.

"God loves us and has a wonderful plan for our life." The good news of our common life gives us identity and community, a history and a future. But that, too, is swallowed up by a yet greater and more important truth.

"God loves the world and has a wonderful plan for the cosmos." He gave his Son to transform everything. He calls each of us, all of us, to join in the transformation.

We walk in the steps of Jesus, translating his gospel into ever-new situations. We expect to grow together and multiply until we meet Jesus and the resurrection of everything. Then he and his redeemed creation will no longer be a bubble of hope in an alien world. We will be all in all.

DISCUSSION GUIDE

By Kristi Reimer

SESSION 1
THE DECEPTIVELY FAMILIAR JESUS (CHAPTER 1)

1. What did you think about Jesus when you were young?

2. How has your view of him changed over the years?

3. In what ways has the change been due to influences of culture, and in what ways has it been due to your changing understanding of Scripture?

4. What are some of the more ambiguous or startling accounts from Jesus' life as reported in the Gospels?

5. What stories have especially puzzled you and why?

6. The author compares studying Jesus to studying Abraham Lincoln: we could study Lincoln's wisdom outside the context of the Civil War, as has often been done with Jesus outside his context (pp. 12-13). What do we miss in taking this approach, with Lincoln and with Jesus?

7. The author contrasts personal spirituality—being "a religious consumer who gets pleasurable spiritual experiences through Christ"—with Christ's mission in the context of Israel's history

(pp. 13-15). How are these ideas compatible, and how do they conflict?

SESSION 2
WHY REPENTANCE? FOR WHAT SINS? (CHAPTERS 2 AND 3)

1. Can you identify with the author when he says, "I never really understood John [the Baptist], and I certainly didn't see why the Gospels began Jesus' ministry by telling about John"? Why or why not?

2. If you announced to your neighbors, "The kingdom of heaven is at hand," what would that mean to them? What would you have to explain?

3. Can you think of a time when an announcement completely changed the direction of your life? If so, what was it?

4. Does the idea of sin being "a family affair" strike you as strange?

5. How do your ideas about sin differ from those of ancient Israel, as portrayed by the author?

6. In what ways do you identify with the author as a "church consumer"?

7. What are some steps you can take to identify more fully with the church as a whole?

8. Describe your baptism experience. What did it mean to you then, and what does it mean to you now?

9. The author gives a couple of examples of circumstances—lack of a strong youth program, an ultra-authoritarian pastor—in which it's acceptable to seek out another congregation. What faults and flaws should we tolerate and "bear with" in our local churches, even though we may not like or agree with them?

SESSION 3
JESUS' TEMPTATIONS AND JESUS' MESSAGE (CHAPTERS 4 AND 5)

1. Why does the author say that Jesus' temptation was a natural outgrowth of the baptism of the Holy Spirit (p. 42)?

2. How does this change your attitude toward temptation?

3. Discuss the difference between daily temptations that many of us face and the kind that Satan launched at Jesus (p. 43).

4. What do our temptations tell us about the state of our spiritual life?

5. What surprises you about the way Jesus responded to Satan's temptations?

6. Respond to this statement from the author: "Satan would like us to work with maximum effectiveness at a goal ten degrees off target" (p. 46).

7. How do we see that borne out in our own lives?

8. How did Jesus respond to the "all about me" temptation (p. 46)?

9. What clues does this give us about how we can respond to such temptations?

10. What does Jesus' interaction with Scripture tell us about the role Scripture should play in our lives as we face temptation?

11. How can we "preach" the kingdom of heaven as Jesus did, in a culturally relevant way as opposed to offering vague timeless truths?

12. What is "the Jesus event" that the author refers to (see pp. 72-73), and how do we communicate it to the world?

SESSION 4

PREACHING THE KINGDOM (CHAPTERS 6 AND 7)

1. If God's kingdom blesses the "sick, bedraggled, desperate people" and the "good-hearted people who seem to have no weight in the world," who are these "improbables" in our society today?

   Alternatively, who are the "Greeks and Romans" outside of Israel?

2. Why is getting out of our circle of friends, our ethnic group, our social class uncomfortable?

3. How can we deliberately do this more often with the news of the kingdom?

4. What has your experience been with the "worship wars" or other church fights?

5. How do we deal with these church battles in the context of the kingdom?

6. The author states that Jesus was like a revolutionary in the way he recruited followers (p. 98). What evidence do you see for this in the Gospel accounts?

7. What do you think of the story of John Wimber, whose mentor discouraged him from making a commitment to Christ until he was absolutely sure he could give his whole heart (p. 99)?

8. How might this be an example for us in our own evangelistic efforts?

9. If, as the author states, evangelism is a "group project," how can we become part of a traveling band inviting others to join and less of a lone ranger creating other lone rangers?

10. How do you interpret Jesus' admonition to turn the other cheek?

To give your tunic along with your cloak?

How do these statements apply to the church as a whole?

11. The author observes that the New Testament letter writers spent very little time on evangelism. How does their lack of emphasis on evangelism fit with the obvious mission emphasis of the first-century church?

12. What implications does that have for us today?

SESSION 5
THE EXTREME JESUS (CHAPTERS 8 AND 9)

1. Have you ever asked someone to "follow you" in a particular endeavor? What was that experience like?

2. The author states that only Jesus has the authority to call people "to quit their work, to leave their families," and so on (p. 111). In what ways do we sometimes confuse our role with Jesus'?

3. Who do you know who has answered a "radical call" to follow Christ? Describe that person.

4. How has your local church nurtured (or not) Christ's calling on individual lives?

5. Have you ever witnessed or experienced miraculous healing or some other act of divine power? If so, describe that experience.

6. What do you think Jesus meant when, after an extensive display of his healing power, he told John the Baptist's disciples in Luke 7:23, "Blessed is the man who does not fall away on account of me" (p. 123)?

7. Jesus sent out his followers to heal and to cast out demons (Luke 10). Followers of Christ today rarely perform such dramatic acts.

(Or, if they do, they're often viewed with considerable skepticism.) Why do you think this is?

8. What are your thoughts on prayers for healing? Should they be public or private?

9. What should Christians expect when they pray for healing?

10. What are some "natural wonders" that we are called to do as Christ's followers?

SESSION 6
PRAYING AND WARNINGS (CHAPTERS 10 AND 11)

1. How do you spend most of your time in prayer?

2. In what ways can we pray more deliberately from a kingdom and family perspective than from an individualistic point of view?

3. What does "our daily bread" entail beyond physical needs?

4. The author mentions racism and exclusion as corporate debts for which the church needs to ask and receive forgiveness (p. 144). What are some others?

5. Are there any of Jesus' words or actions that you find particularly "abrasive" (p. 148)?

6. Name some of the groups of people that Jesus warned, either directly or through his parables.

   Who might be considered the present-day equivalents of these groups and why?

7. What is your reaction to the passage from Jonathan Edwards's "Sinners in the Hands of an Angry God" (pp. 151-52)?

8. If, as the author states, the gospel is not a "'timeless truth,' avail-

able at our convenience" (p. 152), what is it?

SESSION 7
THE FINAL WEEK (CHAPTERS 12, 13 AND 14)

1. The author writes, "Jerusalem was all that Paris is to the French, London is to the English, and Washington, D.C., is to the Americans. It was Rome to Catholics and the Ganges River to Hindus" (p. 163). What do you think might be your "Jerusalem"?

2. Based on Jesus' actions, when is it appropriate to act in righteous anger (such as Christ's protest at the temple), and when should we act in humility and love (his nonresistance to the Roman authorities)?

3. In chapter thirteen, the author mentions Christ's temple protest, his refashioning of the Passover meal, his ride into Jerusalem on a donkey and washing his disciples' feet as symbolic acts. Why did Jesus use symbolic actions rather than just saying what he meant?

4. If you celebrated the Lord's Supper (or Eucharist or Communion) growing up, what did it mean to you? What does it mean to you now?

5. How are we called to be symbol makers like Jesus?

6. What are some symbolic acts that you have witnessed or participated in?

7. Can you recount a time of "bottomless sorrow" in your life? What effect did that grief have on your prayer life?

8. What is your reaction to betrayal or abandonment by friends? What was Jesus' reaction? How can our actions become more like his?

9. What happens when Christians ignore dark emotions of despair and pain?

10. What was Jesus' solution in his darkest hour (pp. 202-3)?

SESSION 8
RESURRECTION LIFE (CHAPTERS 15 AND 16)

1. What did resurrection mean to the Jews in Jesus' day?

2. What does it mean for Christians today?

3. According to the author, a popular version of the gospel is "God forgives our sins so that we can go to heaven when we die" (p. 220). What's right about this statement? What's wrong with it?

4. What do you see as your role in the movement Jesus started in A.D. 30?

5. If it's true that the gospel has an independent power that does not depend on human beings (p. 226), how do we see that independent power at work?

6. Which aspect of Jesus' life do you identify the most with and find it easiest to follow (p. 232)?

   Which do you find it difficult to identify with and struggle to emulate?

7. How does the church succeed in its role as the resurrected body, and how does it sometimes fail?

   How should we respond to its failures?

8. Describe a person you've known who seemed to be brimming with "resurrection life."

9. If you were asked, "Where can I see resurrection life?" what would you say?

ACKNOWLEDGMENTS

As always, I rely on friends. A number were generous to read earlier drafts of this work and give me comments: Harold Fickett, Philip Yancey, Anthony LeDonne, Paul Gullixson, Mark Labberton, Fred Prudek and Michael Griffin. All of them offered valuable comments. Katie, Chase and Popie Stafford also read manuscripts at various stages and talked me through the material. It is a unique joy to have those whom I love so deeply share in the work that means so much to me. Andy Le Peau, my editor at IVP, has been a wise and balanced sounding board, reading several versions of this book while helping it find its present form. I am grateful to have him and the entire group at IVP as colleagues.

NOTES

Chapter 2
page 20   "These statements": N. T. Wright, *Jesus and the Victory of God* (Minneapolis: Fortress, 2002), p. 226.
page 23   The Roman historian Josephus: N. T. Wright, *The New Testament and the People of God* (Minneapolis: Fortress, 1992), p. 176.

Chapter 3
pages 38-39 Lewis Tappan was: Bertram Wyatt-Brown, *Lewis Tappan and the Evangelical War Against Slavery* (Baton Rouge: Louisiana State University Press, 1997).
page 39   U.N. ambassador Andrew Young: Andrew Young, *An Easy Burden: The Civil Rights Movement and the Transformation of America* (New York: HarperCollins, 1996), p. 135.

Chapter 4
page 46   "He was reminding Jesus": Ajith Fernando, *Jesus Driven Ministry* (Wheaton, Ill.: Crossway, 2002), p. 75.
page 52   As a young girl: Corrie ten Boom, *The Hiding Place* (Uhrichsville, Ohio: Barbour, 1987), p. 33.
page 58   "I've made an agreement": Marilee Dunker, *Man of Vision, Woman of Prayer* (Nashville: Thomas Nelson, 1980), p. 149.
page 61   "He'll be coming": C. S. Lewis, *The Lion, the Witch and the Wardrobe* (New York: Macmillan, 1950), p. 182.
page 63   "When I see": Fernando, *Jesus Driven Ministry*, pp. 78-79.

Chapter 5
page 71   "The whole point": N. T. Wright, *Jesus and the Victory of God* (Minneapolis: Fortress, 2002), p. 228.

Chapter 6
page 84   All around Jesus: Dallas Willard, *The Divine Conspiracy: Rediscovering Our Hidden Life in God* (San Francisco: HarperSanFrancisco, 1998), p. 97.

Chapter 7
page 99   "I can remember": Tod Bolsinger, in an interview with the author, January 2004.
page 105   "How can this strange story": Lesslie Newbigin, *Word in Season* (Grand Rapids: Eerdmans, 1994), p. 42.

Chapter 8
page 112 Of twenty-seven Church Missionary Society missionaries: Andrew Walls, *The Missionary Movement in Christian History* (Maryknoll, N.Y.: Orbis, 1996), p. 171.

Chapter 9
page 118 Four hundred baptized Christians: Tim Stafford, "India Undaunted," *Christianity Today*, May 2004, p. 30.
page 135 Through Philip's eyes: Paul Brand and Philip Yancey, *In the Likeness of God* (Grand Rapids: Zondervan, 2004), pp. 11-26.

Chapter 11
page 151 "Being in the hands of God": George Marsden, *Jonathan Edwards* (New Haven: Yale University Press, 2003), p. 222.

Chapter 12
page 171 "Now I'm praying for revival in the whole area!": Tim Stafford, "The Joy of Suffering in Sri Lanka," *Christianity Today,* October 2003, pp. 58-59.
page 174 Crouch notes InterVarsity's: Andy Crouch, "Campus Collisions," *Christianity Today*, October 2003, p. 60.

Chapter 14
page 193 "Ordinary men": W. H. Lewis, ed., *Letters of C. S. Lewis* (New York: Harcourt, Brace & World, 1966), pp. 190-91.
page 196 According to Barna Research: Tim Stafford, "The Church: Why Bother?" *Christianity Today*, January 2005, pp. 42-49.
page 204 "We always get asked": Tim Stafford, "India Undaunted," *Christianity Today*, May 2004, pp. 34-35.

Chapter 15
page 206 The Gospel accounts cannot: N. T. Wright, *The Resurrection of the Son of God* (Minneapolis: Fortress, 2003).
page 208 "No doubt the words": Andrew Walls, *The Missionary Movement in Christian History* (Maryknoll, N.Y.: Orbis, 1996), p. 17.
page 212 The majority of Jews: Wright, *The Resurrection of the Son of God*, p. 129.
page 217 "A messiah who was executed": Ibid., p. 485.
page 218 At least one first-century rebel: N. T. Wright, *Jesus and the Victory of God* (Minneapolis: Fortress, 2002), p. 468.
page 219 "Gentlemen, this is one time": John Rodman Paul, *A History of Poliomyelitis* (New Haven, Conn.: Yale University Press, 1971), p. 260.
page 219 "Flushed by the first report": Jane Smith, *Patenting the Sun: Polio and the Salk Vaccine* (New York: W. Morrow, 1990), p. 319. For the history of polio, see also Nina Seavey, Jane Smith and Paul Wagner, *A Paralyzing Fear: The Triumph over Polio in America* (New York: TV Books, 1998), and Edmund J. Sass, *Polio's Legacy: An Oral History* (Lanham, Md.: University Press of America, 1996).

Chapter 16
page 227 "There's plenty of truth": Gil Bailie, *Violence Unveiled* (New York: Crossroad, 1995), p. 20.

page 229   Christianity spreads through translation: Andrew Walls, *The Missionary Movement in Christian History* (Maryknoll, N.Y.: Orbis, 1996), pp. 26-42.

page 231   "The Maori responded to the gospel": Andrew Walls, *The Cross-Cultural Process in Christian History* (Maryknoll, N.Y.: Orbis, 2002), p. 23.